Relish

OUR HAND PICKED RESTAURANTS

Relish
RESTAURANT REWARDS

As the proud owner of a Relish cookbook, you may subscribe for your own personal Relish Rewards card which entitles you to free membership for one year.

You can access the Relish members' area on our website and find out what exclusive offers are available to you from the fantastic restaurants featured in our series of books throughout the UK.

SUBSCRIBE FOR YOUR REWARD CARD ON OUR HOMEPAGE
Simply register your name, address and title of Relish book purchased to receive your **FREE Relish Reward Card**
www.relishpublications.co.uk

When you make a reservation, simply let the restaurant know that you are a member and take your card along with you.

WHAT ARE THE REWARDS?
The rewards will continue to be updated on the website so do check and keep in touch. These range from a free bottle of Champagne to free gifts when you dine. Relish will send you a quarterly newsletter with special discounts, rewards and free recipes. We are about quality not quantity!

All offers are subject to change. See the Relish website for details.

www.relishpublications.co.uk

004
CONTENTS

006
CONTENTS

Ballotine of Ham Hock, Smoked Pineapple, Carrot Jelly, Crispy Feta, Balsamic Raisins - **Page 042**

009
STARTERS

011
MAINS

Evesham Strawberries, Elderflower & Mascarpone, Mint - Page 136

013
DESSERTS

015
FOREWORD BY ADAM STOKES

Cooking is very important to me. I live my life by it. I even choose holiday destinations around restaurant visits. I grew up in the Midlands knowing what real food tasted like. My dad had (and still has) an allotment where all of the family's vegetables were grown; we had a constant supply of broad beans, carrots, tomatoes and onions to name but a few. I learnt what food is meant to taste like... We had carrots picked on a Sunday morning delivered next to the roast for lunch, onions and shallots drying in the garage and broad bean parties. I was surrounded by so much fresh food I couldn't help but grow up loving the stuff!

My professional career began at Hambleton Hall when I was aged 18, fresh-faced and straight out of catering college. I started on the garnish section as a commis and over the next seven years worked my way up to sous chef alongside head chef Aaron Patterson. From its rural location, the focus was on butchery, seasonality, food marriages and seasoning. Following the completion of my progression at Hambleton, I took the head chef position at Glenapp Castle in 2008. Along with my wife Natasha, I spent the next five years in Scotland where we achieved a Michelin Star and 4 AA Rosettes putting the restaurant in the top three in Scotland and the top 30 in the country.

In 2013 we moved back to the Midlands and created Adam's with our aim being to offer good cooking and modern dining to Birmingham. We have a more informal feel to the restaurant where guests can relax, chat, eat, drink and spend a few hours with friends, colleagues or loved ones. The Midlands' larder is an interesting one; on the surface it seems to be a bit sparse but when you start to crack through the surface, you find small artisan producers of cheese and bread, passionate family-run meat and fish companies, local shot game as well as growers of fruit, vegetables and unique herbs.

We now have an extremely diverse food scene in the Midlands, from street food to fine dining, with Birmingham holding more Michelin stars than any other city outside London and I am very proud to be a part of that.

Relish Midlands is a fantastic recipe book that brings together so many of the talented chefs and quality restaurants in the area. It gives you a taste of what our exciting region has to offer and a peek into the culinary delights available, as well as the encouragement to try some new recipes.

Adam Stokes, Adam's

016

A CULINARY JOURNEY THROUGH THE MIDLANDS

'The Second City', they call it. And Birmingham's not joking. With the exception of London, there is no place like Brum when it comes to Great British food. The city boasts 5 Michelin stars and has rapidly emerged as a European centre of excellence. Perhaps it's time to change its nickname. These days, 'Gourmetville' seems more appropriate.

A journey around the Midlands culinary hotspots inevitably starts in the 'Second City'. The starry skills of Adam Stokes and wife Natasha are on display at the chef's eponymously-named restaurant, Adam's, which is located in Bennetts Hill. An impressive interior makes way for spellbinding and delicate food, which fully deserves its Top 30 Restaurant ranking from the Good Food Guide. With impressive tasting menus that run to three, five or nine courses, British dining in the heart of Birmingham doesn't come any finer.

The venerable Simpsons, at Edgbaston, has for many years been the city's standard-bearer. It has retained its star for some 16 years, a remarkable testament to the quality, consistency and drive of chef Luke Tipping and his team. Tipping used to run the kitchen with his long-standing chef friend Adam Bennett, a Bocuse d'Or challenger who creates impeccably refined food. In recent times, Bennett has moved to The Cross, at Kenilworth, winning a Michelin star along the way for dishes that are built around the finest local, seasonal ingredients. Cheal's of Henley is the newest kid on the block; an elegant restaurant run by former Simpsons' chef Matt Cheal. Luke, Adam and Matt owe much to Andreas Antona, the owner of both Simpsons and The Cross and a much-loved Godfather figure in the West Midlands.

While Birmingham now takes all the plaudits, Ludlow, in nearby Shropshire, continues to punch above its weight. The picturesque market town, described by former Poet Laureate Sir John Betjeman as being the 'loveliest' in England, has an indelible association with great food.

A wonderful food festival, exceptional farmers market and collection of great restaurants keep it ahead of the crowd. The Charlton Arms, run by Cedric Bosi, brother of the 2 Michelin starred former Ludlow resident Claude Bosi, offers great food in informal surrounds.
The fast-rising Fishmore Hall serves classical British dishes with strong French influences under the tutelage of the exceptional young Andrew Birch, who learned his trade under the Michelin starred Matthew Tompkinson at The Montagu Arms, on the south coast. Nearby, chef Karl Martin has catapulted Old Downton Lodge to the forefront of diners' imagination. His highly creative food is rooted in the natural resources undulating South Shropshire has to offer. He forages daily during his walk to work and serves cutting edge food in stately surrounds. Little wonder tongues are wagging about his culinary prowess.

Ludlow is no longer the only gastronomic hotspot in Shropshire. The extravagantly pretty county has a delightful market town, Shrewsbury, which has enjoyed a renaissance in recent years. The Pound Inn, at Leebotwood, on its outskirts, is a highly recommended gastro pub that serves robustly flavoursome food. One of the region's most creative chefs, the talented Chris Burt, oversees three Shrewsbury restaurants, Momo No Ki, The Peach Tree and Havana Republic, which offer the best of global cuisine. Burt is in tune with emerging flavours and creates new, off-the-cuff dishes on a daily basis.

Reputations in the neighbouring West Midlands have risen in recent years and that's no surprise. Chefs like Steve Kirkham, at The Fairlawns Hotel and Spa in Walsall, have been driving up standards with passion and determination. Further east, in nearby Lichfield, ambitious head chef Paul Proffitt is taking on the world, one plate at a time. He has an exceptional natural larder on his doorstep, with 80 Sika deer roaming in meadows and woodland and a remarkable walled garden. Proffitt cooks dreamy, artistic plates at Swinfen, an idyllic 18th Century manor that is quintessentially English.

The Belfry is equally impressive. Renowned as one of the leading golfing venues in the world, it has hosted the Ryder Cup on four occasions and staged numerous European Tour events. Its à la carte menu from chef director Glen Watson offers locally sourced, freshly selected and lovingly prepared food.

Further north, Thoresby Hall Hotel is a Grade 1 19th Century country house set in 30 acres of gardens created by Humphry Repton. Its newly-refurbished Blue Grill offers a 2 AA Rosette menu in one of the region's most impressive dining rooms.

From Thoresby, it's a picturesque drive to two eastern restaurants, the delightful Old Bakery at Lincoln, where Tracey and Ivano de Serio serve contemporary, Italian inspired dishes, and the picturesque Cherry House in Peterborough, a long established and much-loved, thatched roof restaurant that chef/patron Andrew Corrick has fashioned in his own image.

A circuitous route back towards Birmingham leads via four stand-out restaurants. Restaurant 23 at Leamington Spa is the vision of highly rated chef/patron Peter Knibb, a Claridge's and Chez Nico alumni, whose precision cooking has made overtures to Michelin inspectors.

The Lygon Arms, at Broadway in Worcester, is further south, in a chocolate box village hewn from golden coloured stone. The 16th Century building, set in three acres, boasts classic cuisine with an impressive wine list. Buckland Manor is also a remarkable manor house, located in the nearby Cotswolds. Situated next to a church and in ten acres of gardens, its breathtaking location is matched only by the delectable fine dining from multi award-winning chef William Guthrie. Thereafter, heading back north towards Kidderminster, The Plough Inn is an inviting and comfortable pub restaurant offering à la carte dining and an Aga carvery; perfect for Sunday lunch.

All roads lead back to Birmingham, a city that offers so much more than fine dining. A vibrant and eclectic restaurant scene is embodied by the city's bright and breezy new Spanish restaurant, El Borracho de Oro, created by Emma Yufera-Ruiz. Her new venue, the result of a ten year dream, has added sparkle and pizzazz to the leafy suburb of Edgbaston.

Sensational produce, starry dining rooms and high functioning chefs; the Midlands has it all. Take time to Relish what's in store.

Andy Richardson, Relish Food Photographer
www.awaywithmedia.com

018
ADAM'S

16 Waterloo Street, Birmingham, B2 5UG (from Jan 2016)

0121 643 3745
www.adamsrestaurant.co.uk Twitter: @RestaurantAdams Facebook: Adam's Restaurant

A dam's opened in 2013 as a 'pop up' restaurant in Birmingham city centre and within the first six months received a string of nationally recognised awards from a Michelin star to 3 AA Rosettes. This small, eponymous restaurant sprang up in an old sandwich shop in the heart of Birmingham's thriving business and shopping district.

Adam's has proved a huge success, so much so that in early 2016 husband and wife team Adam and Natasha Stokes expanded round the corner on Waterloo Street. Extensive renovation of three floors of New Oxford House has allowed for an exciting expansion. Adam's boasts more dining space as well as a chef's table, open kitchen, glazed wine room and a development kitchen.

Adam's has become a landmark venue within the gastronomic landscape of Birmingham, serving modern British food in a comfortable and relaxed setting.

The aim is to create an experience unique for each diner, informal but elegant and without the traditional rules of fine dining. There is an absence of tablecloths and no required dress code, just professional and approachable service. Adam's trademark tasting menu will be on offer alongside varied menus of seasonal and ever evolving dishes for guests to sample.

Modern and stylish Michelin starred cooking in the centre of Birmingham. 'Our aim is to take you through a culinary journey of tastes and textures.' Adam Stokes.

DUCK HEARTS, FENNEL, BROAD BEANS

SERVES 4

🍷 *2012 Blaufrankisch, Hopler, Burgenland (Austria)*

Ingredients

Duck Hearts

20 duck hearts
75g salt
750ml water
5g star anise
5g orange zest
4g thyme

Red Wine Sauce

300ml red wine
100ml port
150g veal glace

Onion Purée

250g white onion (sliced)
2½g thyme
30g butter
200ml milk
150ml chicken stock
180ml double cream
5½g gellan gum

Vegetables

1kg broad beans (in pods)
150g hen-of-the-wood mushrooms

Garnish

20g wild rice
100ml vegetable oil
micro parsley
100g bulb fennel

Method

For The Duck Hearts (Prepare ahead)

Slice the bottom off each of the hearts and remove the membrane. Mix the water, salt, star anise, orange zest and thyme together to make a brine, then immerse the hearts in the brine for 6 hours. Rinse off with fresh water, pat dry and place in a sealed container in the fridge. They will last for up to 3 days.

For The Red Wine Sauce

Bring the red wine and port to the boil to allow the alcohol to evaporate. Add the veal glace and continue to boil until reduced to a sauce consistency.

For The Onion Purée

Sweat the onions with the butter and thyme until soft. Add the milk, chicken stock and cream, then simmer for 10 minutes. Lightly blend and pass through a sieve. Add the gellan gum to the liquor and blend with a hand held blender. Cool the liquor over a bowl of ice until set, then return back to the food processor and blend until smooth.

For The Vegetables

Remove the beans from the pods, *blanch* in salted, boiling water, remove swiftly and refresh in ice cold water. Remove the dull, rubbery outer shell of the beans to leave the bright green inside.

Wash the mushrooms thoroughly, pat dry and set aside until ready to use.

For The Garnish

Heat the vegetable oil up to 245°C and carefully add in the wild rice - it will puff instantly. Remove and drain on kitchen paper.

Remove the 'petals' from the fennel bulb and slice extremely thinly on a mandolin. Reserve until needed.

To Assemble The Dish

Heat the purée, broad beans and the red wine sauce. Quickly fry the duck hearts and hen-of-the-wood mushrooms together until golden. Slice the hearts in half and arrange them on the plate. Neatly arrange the purée, broad beans and hen-of-the-woods around the hearts. Carefully place the puffed wild rice, fennel and micro parsley on top of the hearts and mushrooms. Finish with a light drizzle of sauce.

Chef's Tip

This dish is a great way to start a meal as it is tasty and interesting. To make it into a lunchtime dish, toss over salad leaves and serve with sourdough bread and a good quality butter.

HALIBUT, LEEKS, OREGANO, BROWN SHRIMPS

SERVES 4

2013 Grüner Veltliner, Erich Machherndl, Wachau (Austria)

Ingredients

Fish

1kg halibut fillet
100g brown shrimps
50g shallots
15g butter
3g garlic
5g chives
lemon (squeeze of, optional)

Leek Sauce

300g leeks (roughly chopped)
50g butter
200ml chicken stock
75ml whipping cream

Oregano Oil

50g oregano leaves
50ml pomace olive oil

Vegetables

75g sea purslane
75g sea aster
75g shiitake mushrooms
butter (2 knobs of)

Method

For The Fish

Remove all skin and sinew from the halibut and cut into 4 equal portions. Keep in the fridge until required.

Melt the butter and soften the shallots and garlic over a low heat. Add the shrimps and chives and keep warm.

For The Leek Sauce

Quickly sauté the leeks with the butter until translucent. Add the chicken stock and cream, then boil quickly for 10 minutes. Blend well in a food processor, pass through a sieve and keep warm.

For The Oregano Oil

Pick the leaves from the oregano and *blanch* very quickly in salted, boiling water. Refresh in iced water and dry. Blend with the pomace oil. Keep in the fridge.

For The Vegetables

Carefully pick through the vegetables removing any stalks and unwanted leaves. Wash thoroughly and cook for a couple of minutes in water and butter until soft.

Slice the shiitake mushrooms and fry in butter until soft.

To Assemble The Dish

Gently grill the halibut, turning every 30 seconds to stop it drying out, for 5 minutes under the grill, then allow to rest fully. Cook for another 2 minutes, turning at least every 30 seconds.

Spiral the leek sauce on the plate and place the halibut to one side. Add a few shrimps over the top, then add the sea vegetables and shiitake mushrooms. Finish with a little oregano oil. Serve immediately.

Chef's Tip

Give the fish a good squeeze of lemon juice after it is cooked to really help the flavour of the fish sing.

RASPBERRY, LEMON VERBENA, ALMONDS

SERVES 4

🍷 *NV Demi Sec, Nyetimber, Chiltington (England)*

Ingredients

Raspberry Meringue

150g raspberry purée
20g dried egg white

Raspberry Sorbet

850g raspberries
100g caster sugar
35g Sosa neutral acid (or citric acid)

Lemon Verbena Cream

200ml full-fat milk
1 egg
1 egg yolk
75g caster sugar
25g cornflour
50g lemon verbena leaves
50g butter
3/4 leaf gelatine (softened)
35ml double cream (lightly whipped)

Raspberry Syrup

raspberries (handful of)
sugar (sprinkling of)
water (splash of)

Garnish

40g freeze dried raspberries
20 raspberries
5g lemon verbena leaves (picked)
20 fresh almonds

Method

For The Raspberry Meringue (Prepare the day before)

Preheat the oven to 90°C.

Mix the raspberry purée and dried egg white together and whisk on full speed in a food processor until light and aerated. Spread over a sheet of silicon paper and dry in the oven for 7 hours, or overnight.

For The Raspberry Sorbet

Break the raspberries in a sieve with a ladle to make a thick purée. Add the sugar and the neutral acid, taste and churn in an ice cream machine. When set, store in the freezer. Soften slightly just before required. If you have difficulty sourcing the neutral or citric acid, you may use the same quantity of fresh lemon juice.

For The Lemon Verbena Cream

Bring the milk to the boil. Whisk the egg, egg yolk, cornflour and caster sugar together, then add the milk and cook on a low heat for 4 minutes. Cool the mix a little, then add the lemon verbena, butter and gelatine. Blend in a food processor until smooth and pass through a sieve. Cool completely, then add the double cream. Place into a piping bag. Refrigerate.

For The Raspberry Syrup

Place the raspberries in a pan with the sugar and a little water. Boil gently until syrupy. Cool, then pass through a sieve ensuring all the juice comes out of the raspberries.

For The Garnish

Remove the almonds from their green husks and use immediately.

To Assemble The Dish

Place sliced, fresh raspberries on the plate and pipe the lemon verbena cream next to the raspberries. Garnish with freeze dried raspberries, raspberry syrup, almonds and the lemon verbena sprigs. Scoop the raspberry sorbet onto the plate and place shards of raspberry meringue on top. Serve immediately.

Chef's Tip

Only make this dish during the English raspberry season. It is good all year round but during the season it is magical!

028
THE BELFRY HOTEL & RESORT, RYDER GRILL

Lichfield Road, Sutton Coldfield, B76 9PR

0844 980 0600
www.thebelfry.co.uk Twitter: @thebelfryhotel Facebook: belfryhotel

Under the ever watchful eye of the award-winning chef director Glen Watson, The Ryder Grill succeeds in providing the most memorable of dining experiences.

Nestled in the heart of The Belfry Hotel and Resort, Sutton Coldfield, this elegant restaurant provides a refreshing take on modern dining. Diners can enjoy stunning views across the iconic Brabazon golf course from The Ryder Grill's outdoor terrace or choose to soak up the atmosphere at the showcase grill as it takes centre stage.

Watson joined The Ryder Grill in 2013 from the Albert Roux Consultancy, transforming the West Midlands resort into a top gastronomic destination with the support of executive chef, Robert Bates and pastry chef, Dean Cole, all instrumental in the launch of The Ryder Grill's à la carte menu.

THE BELFRY
HOTEL & RESORT

The menu has been designed to appeal to an array of palates and provide more exquisite options for guests to enhance their culinary experience. With the showcase grill at the heart of The Ryder Grill, the menu complements the succulent Chateaubriand and aged steaks that diners have come to expect from the Belfry's signature restaurant.

The Ryder Grill caters for all needs and matches the mood of any occasion; guests can enjoy a romantic date night, unwind with a relaxing meal after one of The Belfry's signature spa treatments or simply gather friends after a breathtaking round of golf on one of The Belfry's three courses. Diners can then round off a perfect visit to the Ryder Grill with an overnight stay in one of the hotel's luxurious rooms.

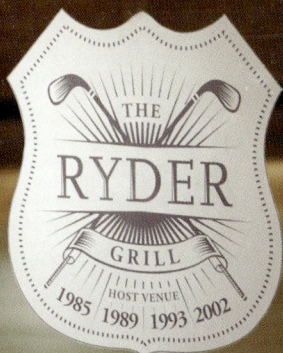

THE
RYDER
GRILL

HOST VENUE
1985 | 1989 | 1993 | 2002

The Belfry Hotel & Resort, named England's Leading Resort 2015, is set in 500 acres of rolling North Warwickshire countryside and is the world's only venue to host The Ryder Cup on four separate occasions.

TUNA TARTAR, CHOPPED AVOCADO, PICKLED GINGER, SESAME SEEDS

SERVES 4

Sancerre Blanc Domaine Vacheron (France)

Ingredients

Tuna Tartar

400g fresh tuna loin
40ml extra virgin olive oil
4g Maldon sea salt

Homemade Pickled Ginger

20g caster sugar
3ml rice vinegar
15ml white wine vinegar
60g fresh ginger (peeled, thinly sliced)

Chopped Avocado

1 black skinned avocado
½ lime (juice of)
salt (to taste)
5g coriander leaf (finely chopped)
1g red chilli (finely chopped)

Avocado And Wasabi Purée

1 black skinned avocado
10g wasabi paste
1 lime (juice of)

Soy Dressing

75ml light soy sauce
50ml mirin
25g Dijon mustard
25ml clear rice vinegar
25g runny honey
50ml sweet soy sauce

To Serve

5g breakfast radish
8g black sesame seeds
8g white sesame seeds
20g homemade pickled ginger
4g Thai basil

4 x 8½cm cooks' rings

Method

For The Tuna Tartar

Dice the tuna into 3mm pieces. Dress with extra virgin olive oil and sea salt.

Chef's Tip

Always buy the freshest, best quality tuna available and keep well chilled until preparation.

For The Homemade Pickled Ginger (Allow 24 hours)

Add all the ingredients to a pan except the ginger. Heat the liquid until the sugar dissolves, then add the ginger. Place in a heat resistant jar and seal until use. Leave to pickle for 24 hours before serving.

For The Chopped Avocado

Place half the avocado into a metal mixing bowl, season with salt and mix with the lime juice. Mash with a fork.

Dice the other half and carefully stir into the mashed avocado along with the coriander and chilli. Check the seasoning and place in the rings, smoothing out the surface. Add the diced tuna on top and lightly press.

Place greaseproof paper on top until required.

For The Avocado And Wasabi Purée

Place the avocado into a mixer with the lime juice and the wasabi paste (to taste). Season and place in a piping bag.

For The Soy Dressing

Combine all the ingredients in a pan. Simmer and reduce by half to a coating consistency.

To Serve

Slice the radish thinly and place on top of the tuna ring, sprinkle with a few black and white sesame seeds. Pipe or *quenelle* the avocado and wasabi purée on top of the tuna. Garnish with the pickled ginger and Thai basil. Place onto a plate and dot the soy dressing around. Serve immediately.

CLASSIC CHATEAUBRIAND WITH CHUNKY CHIPS & SAUCE BEARNAISE

SERVES 4 (each chateaubriand serves 2)

*Callia Lunaris Malbec
(Argentina)*

Ingredients

2 x 650g beef chateaubriand (28 day aged)

Herb Reduction

5g shallots (finely chopped)
20g tarragon (finely chopped)
5g chervil (finely chopped)
60ml white wine vinegar
80ml white wine
2g white peppercorns (wrapped in muslin)

Sauce Béarnaise

250g *clarified* unsalted butter (warmed)
4 egg yolks
10ml white wine vinegar
40ml white wine
¼ lemon
salt (pinch of)

To Serve

360g chunky chips
8 Portobello mushrooms
100g Chanterelle mushrooms (optional)
100g vine cherry tomatoes
100g broccoli
60g asparagus
120g carrots
20g unsalted butter
Maldon sea salt (to taste)

Method

For The Herb Reduction

Wrap the peppercorns in muslin as you want them to infuse only.

Place all the ingredients in a saucepan and bring to a simmer. Reduce until all the moisture has evaporated.

For The Sauce Béarnaise

Place everything, except the butter, in a metal bowl over hot water (*bain-marie*).

Whisk continuously until thick and creamy. Do not let it get too hot or the eggs will 'scramble'.

Add the warm butter whilst still whisking and season. Stir in the herb reduction. Keep warm.

To Cook The Chateaubriand And Serve

Preheat the oven to 190°C (fan).

Season the beef and place in a hot pan with a splash of very hot oil. Turn every minute until fully sealed and golden brown on the outside. Place in the oven and cook for 17 minutes (medium).

Remove from the oven and allow to rest for at least 10 minutes.

Roast the chunky chips until crispy. *Blanch* and cook all the vegetables, ensuring they are well seasoned.

Garnish your plate or wooden board with the tomatoes, vegetables and chunky chips, then slice the beef thickly once rested. Season with salt and serve with the sauce on the side.

Savour and enjoy!

Chef's Tip

To ensure you get the best from your chateaubriand, it is really important that you let the meat rest.

PEACH MELBA CREME BRULEE

SERVES 4

Royal Tokaji Aszú 5 Puttonyos (Hungary)

Ingredients

Peach Melba Crème Brûlée

150ml double cream
115g white peach purée
1 vanilla pod (split)
5 egg yolks
70g caster sugar (or vanilla sugar)

Raspberry And Vanilla White Chocolate Macaron

2 medium egg whites
60g ground almonds
60g icing sugar
28g caster sugar
red food colouring (a few drops of)
freeze dried raspberry pieces

Vanilla And White Chocolate Cream

200ml whipping cream
5 vanilla pods (split)
125g white chocolate

To Finish

60g caster sugar
fresh raspberries
fresh peach (Parisienne balls)
raspberry purée
peach purée
micro mint

4 ramekins

Method

For The Peach Melba Crème Brûlée (Prepare ahead)

Bring the cream, purée and the split vanilla pod to the boil.

Whisk together the yolks and caster sugar, then pour over the boiled liquid. Mix well, strain the mixture and decant into 4 ramekins. Cook in a *bain-marie* at 130°C until set with a slight wobble, for about 30 minutes, giving longer if required. Cool and refrigerate until needed.

For The Raspberry And Vanilla White Chocolate Macaron

Preheat the oven to 140°C (fan).

Combine 1 egg white, the almonds and icing sugar in a large bowl.

Place the second egg white into an electric mixer with a teaspoon of sugar and whisk until white and fluffy. Add the remaining sugar and whisk until it forms a stiff meringue.

Fold the meringue into the almond mixture, add the colouring and pipe onto greaseproof or silicone paper using a medium, plain nozzle. Finish with dried raspberries.

Bake for 25 minutes until you can remove from the paper. Cool.

For The Vanilla And White Chocolate Cream (Prepare the day before)

Bring half the cream to the boil with the split vanilla pods. Remove from the heat, add the white chocolate and mix well. Stir in the remaining cream (leave the vanilla to infuse), mix well and refrigerate overnight.

Remove the vanilla pods and whip the mixture to thicken slightly. Pipe into the half macaron shell and sandwich with a second shell.

This recipe will make more than 4 macarons - freeze any extra for another occasion.

To Finish

Using a blow torch, caramelise the crème brûlée with the caster sugar, then clean off any excess sugar from the ramekin. Arrange the fruit and purées on the plate. Finish with mint and a macaron.

Chef's Tip

Use any fruit purée in season for this crème brûlée recipe.

BUCKLAND MANOR

Near Broadway, Worcestershire, WR12 7LY

01386 852 626
www.bucklandmanor.co.uk Twitter: @Buckland_Manor Facebook: Buckland Manor

Buckland Manor, a member of Relais & Châteaux, is a very special hotel tucked inconspicuously in a tranquil corner of the village of Buckland, nestled next to the ancient village church. In the heart of the Cotswold tourist trail, Buckland is only a few minutes from the much loved town of Broadway, with its pretty high street and eclectic shops. Staying in Buckland you are well placed to discover the wider area of the Cotswolds, Oxford's dreaming spires and the home of Shakespeare, Stratford upon Avon. Explore during the day and return to relax in the luxurious surrounds and most welcoming of Manor Houses. Whether looking for a romantic getaway, somewhere for a special event or celebration, or a quiet escape, this quintessentially English luxury hotel will not disappoint. Once discovered, you will not want to leave.

William Guthrie heads up the kitchen at Buckland Manor and, with such superb cuisine, he has won many accolades over the years. Since joining Buckland Manor, William has achieved 3 AA Rosettes, 4 AA Red Stars for the hotel and in 2015, was awarded 'Best Hotel Restaurant of the Year' at the Cotswold Life Food and Drink Awards. The restaurant continues to attract connoisseurs of fine food and wine from around the world, as menus feature fresh local produce from the neighbouring Vale of Evesham, affectionately known as the market garden of England. Fresh herbs are also grown in the Manor's own grounds and, as you would expect in a house of this heritage, there is a magnificent wine cellar.

Buckland Manor was awarded 3 AA Rosettes in 2014, putting it in the top 10% of AA restaurants in the UK. It also has 4 AA Red Stars, and other industry accolades including being awarded 'Best Hotel Restaurant of the Year' at the Cotswold Life Food and Drink Awards 2015.

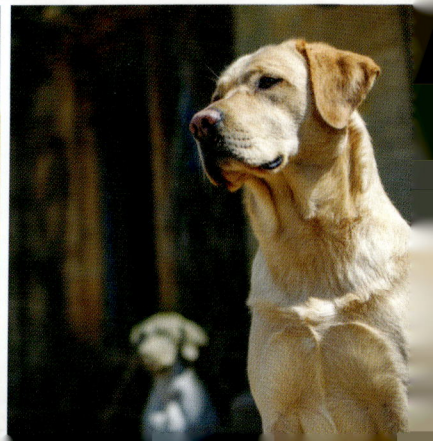

BALLOTINE OF HAM HOCK, SMOKED PINEAPPLE, CARROT JELLY, CRISPY FETA, BALSAMIC RAISINS

SERVES 8

Riesling Kabinett, Joh Jos Prum, Mosel, 2011 (Germany)

Ingredients

Ham Hock
2 ham hocks (washed)
10 litres water
2 onions (1 cut in half, 1 diced)
1 bulb garlic, 2 leeks (chopped)
100g capers (chopped)
100g gherkins (chopped)
100g chives (chopped)
salt and pepper
4 tbsp grain mustard

Balsamic Raisins
100g caster sugar
300ml balsamic vinegar (5 year old)
100g raisins

Carrot Jelly
250ml carrot juice
1½g agar agar, 40g sugar
25g coriander seeds (crushed)
1 leaf gelatine (softened)

Smoked Pineapple
½ pineapple (peeled, halved)
150g rice
100g lapsang tea leaves
50g brown sugar
100ml pineapple juice

Wild Garlic Pesto
100g wild garlic leaf, 5g garlic
50g Parmesan, 50g pine nuts
200ml vegetable oil
salt and pepper (to season)

Crispy Feta
100g feta cheese
50g plain flour, 1 egg (beaten)
100g panko breadcrumbs

Method

For The Ham Hock (Allow 36 hours)

Cover the ham with water in a deep pan. Add the halved onion, garlic and leeks. Cook over a low heat (84°C) for 9 hours. Cool and refrigerate overnight.

Strip the meat off the bones and finely shred.

Sauté the diced onion and mix with the ham hock, capers, gherkins and chives. Season with salt and pepper, then add the grain mustard.

Tightly roll into cylinders using double folded cling film and allow to sit in the fridge for 6 hours.

For The Balsamic Raisins (Prepare the day before)

Bring all the ingredients to a simmer, remove from the heat and *macerate* overnight.

For The Carrot Jelly

Boil the carrot juice, agar, sugar and coriander seeds for 1 minute. Stir in the gelatine, then strain through a fine sieve and set in a small tray to ½cm deep. Cut to required size when needed.

To Smoke The Pineapple

Combine the rice, tea and sugar in a smoking tray and heat until smoking. Place the pineapple in the smoker for 14 minutes for maximum flavour. Transfer into a vacuum pack bag, add the pineapple juice and compress. Alternatively, allow the pineapple to soak in the juice until you're ready to serve.

For The Wild Garlic Pesto

Blanch the wild garlic leaf. Blitz the remaining ingredients to a purée, then add the garlic leaf. Continue puréeing to a fine, green purée.

For The Crispy Feta

Dice the feta into small cubes, *pane*, then deep fry at 160°C until crispy.

To Serve

Serve as pictured.

(see glossary)

LOIN OF TODDINGTON LAMB, SWEETBREAD & ROSEMARY JUS

SERVES 4

🍷 *Côte-Rôtie, Francois et Fils, Northern Rhone, 2010 (France)*

Ingredients

Lamb
1 loin of lamb
300ml local rapeseed oil (we use Cotswold Gold)
1 clove garlic (chopped)
1 sprig rosemary (chopped)
50g butter

Sweetbread
50g sweetbread (soaked overnight in 100ml milk)
50g panko breadcrumbs
1 egg (beaten)
30g plain flour

Rosemary Jus
1kg lamb carcasses
50ml non scented oil
2 large onions (cut into thick rings)
1 bulb garlic (cut in half)
2 sprigs thyme
5 large sprigs rosemary
30ml Armagnac
1 litre chicken stock
200ml veal glace
10g white peppercorns
salt (to season)

Pea Purée
200g frozen peas
2 shallots (chopped)
1 clove garlic (chopped)
100g butter

Herb Crust (combine ingredients)
50g dry breadcrumbs
50g parsley (finely chopped)
25ml oil

Accompaniments
seasonal vegetables

Garnish
herbs, pea shoots

Method

For The Lamb (Prepare the day before)

Marinate the lamb in the oil, garlic and rosemary for 24 hours, or overnight. Place the lamb in a bag and cook in a water bath at 48°C for 30 minutes.

Seal the lamb in a hot pan with the butter. Cook for 8-10 minutes. Alternatively, seal for 2 minutes on each side, then place in the oven at 180°C for a few minutes.

For The Sweetbread

Wash the sweetbread, then *blanch* for 30 seconds. Plunge into iced water for 10 seconds, then peel off the fat and sinew. Roll in the flour, egg and panko breadcrumbs, coating well. Deep fry at 180°C to a light golden colour.

For The Rosemary Jus

Lightly colour the lamb bones in the oil. Add the onion rings and lightly colour, then add in the garlic, thyme and rosemary. Deglaze with the Armagnac, then add the stock, veal glace and peppercorns. Bring to the boil, then simmer for 30 minutes Pass through a colander, then a *chinois* and return to the pan. Reduce to a sauce consistency, *clarifying* as you go. Correct the seasoning, then pass through a muslin cloth.

For The Pea Purée

Defrost the frozen peas and remove the skins.

Sauté the shallots and garlic in butter without colouring. When soft, add the peas and enough water to just cover. Cook quickly until just soft. Season, then blend to a purée. Pass through a sieve.

To Serve

Cook the seasonal vegetables until tender. Press the herb crust on top of the lamb.

Serve as pictured finishing with the herbs, pea shoots and finally, the rosemary jus.

> **Chef's Tip**
> Make sure you take your time and taste, taste, taste to get the best end product!

RASPBERRY DELICE, POPPY SEED MERINGUE, YOGHURT ICE CREAM

SERVES 6

Recioto Classico, Giovanni Allegrini, Veneto, 2009 (Italy)

Ingredients

Yoghurt Ice Cream

750g yoghurt
65g milk powder
325ml full-fat milk
340g caster sugar
90ml double cream

Italian And Poppy Seed Meringue

200g sugar
100ml water
4 egg whites
50g poppy seeds

Raspberry Delice

375g raspberry purée
5 gelatine leaves (softened)
375ml double cream (semi-whipped)
375g *Italian meringue* mix (see above)

Raspberry Jelly

100g raspberry purée
15g sugar
1 leaf gelatine (softened)

Raspberry Gel

250g raspberry purée
2½g agar agar
50g caster sugar

Garnish

fresh raspberries
25g pistachio crumb
dehydrated raspberries (optional)

6 x 5cm moulds

Method

For The Yoghurt Ice Cream (Prepare ahead)

Whisk all the ingredients together, then pass through a fine sieve. Place in a paco jet container and freeze for 12 hours. Churn to order. Alternatively, churn in an ice cream machine and freeze.

For The Italian And Poppy Seed Meringue (Prepare ahead)

Make a stock syrup with the sugar and water. Whisk the egg whites to soft peak and, while still whisking, slowly trickle in the stock syrup. Continue whisking until cool. Set aside 375g.

Spread the remaining mix onto baking paper and dust with poppy seeds. Dehydrate at 110°C for 8 hours. Break into shards.

For The Raspberry Delice

Warm the raspberry purée and dissolve the gelatine into it. When cooled, fold in the reserved 375g of *Italian meringue* and the semi-whipped cream.

Place in desired moulds, and allow to set in the fridge for 2 hours.

For The Raspberry Jelly

Gently warm the purée with the sugar until dissolved. Stir in the gelatine. Set a thin layer on top of the delice.

For The Raspberry Gel

Boil the purée with the agar agar and sugar. Allow to set on a tray. Once set, place in blender and purée to a fine gel.

To Serve

Remove the delice from the moulds and plate up with the other elements. Garnish with raspberries, pistachio crumb and broken shards of dried poppy seed meringue.

> **Chef's Tip**
>
> All elements of this dessert can be made the day prior to service.

(see glossary)

048
THE CHARLTON ARMS

Ludford Bridge, Ludlow, Shropshire, SY8 1PJ

01584 872 813
www.thecharltonarms.co.uk Twitter: @TheCharltonArms

Located in one of the most idyllic settings of any Midlands restaurant, The Charlton Arms in Ludlow stands on the banks of the River Teme at Ludford Bridge and offers stunning views of one of England's prettiest townscapes.

In the foreground, the Teme burbles and tumbles over the nearby weir. In the mid distance, there are views to Ludlow's Medieval Castle and to St Laurence's Church, which is ranked as one of the 20 most beautiful in the country.

Such a backdrop is the perfect setting for French inspired bistro classics, created by husband and wife owners Cedric and Amy Bosi. They acquired The Charlton Arms after a long journey that took in Cedric's native Lyon, in France, his brother Claude's 2 Michelin starred former Ludlow restaurant, Hibiscus, and a number of acclaimed pub-restaurants and hotels in London, Ireland and Herefordshire.

"I came to Ludlow to work for my brother initially," says Cedric. "I wanted to improve my English and asked him for a job. My parents ran their own bistro, so we grew up around great food. I had a little spell in the kitchen, but it wasn't for me. I always preferred front of house."

The Charlton Arms is a charming and picturesque venue that combines a family run freehouse with real ales and fantastic food. There is a spacious and light restaurant and nine en-suite rooms, many with fantastic views. Temptingly tasty breakfasts, delicious dinners and fabulous lunches are available each day using ingredients brought from Ludlow and its hinterland.

THE CHARLTON ARMS

This 4 AA star accommodation with its Rosette awarded restaurant is low on pretence and big on flavour. "It's our recipe for success," says Cedric. "C'est magnifique."

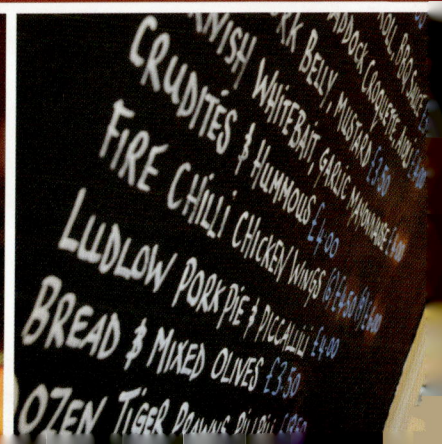

LUDLOW
BREWING CO

GREAT BEER, NATURALLY

CRUDITÉS & HUMMOUS £4.00
FIRE CHILLI CHICKEN WINGS 6/£4.50 12/£8.00
LUDLOW PORK PIE & PICCALILI £4.00
BREAD & MIXED OLIVES £3.50
OZEN TIGER PRAWNS

FRESH TUNA & QUAIL EGG SALAD NICOISE

SERVES 6

Saint Chinian Domaine Belles Courbes (France)
Any strong, dry, Southern French rosé goes well
with this dish.

Ingredients

Tuna

6 large fresh tuna steaks (or 12 small)
extra olive oil

Quail Egg Salad Niçoise

24 quail eggs
1kg baby new potatoes (scrubbed)
600g green beans (topped, tailed)
24 baby tomatoes (wiped, halved)
1 small red onion (very finely sliced)
24 black olives (pitted)
3 tbsp fresh parsley (chopped)
salt and freshly ground black pepper (to taste)
12 anchovy fillets (drained, halved)
3 tbsp virgin olive oil
2 tbsp lemon juice
1 large clove garlic (peeled, crushed)

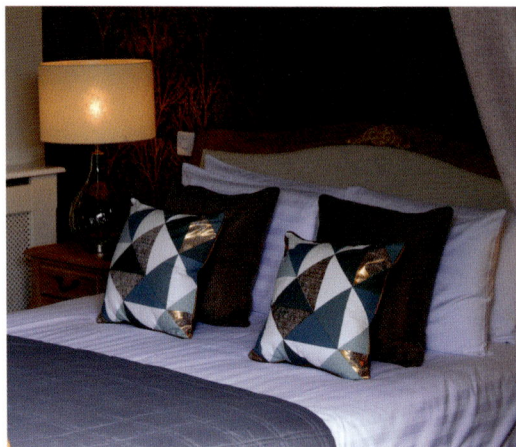

Method

For The Quail Egg Salad Niçoise

Boil the quail eggs for 3 minutes in boiling water, then transfer
to cold water.

Cook the potatoes in salted, boiling water until just soft. Drain
and put in a large dish.

Cook the beans, ensuring that they remain crunchy. Drain, refresh
under cold water and mix with the potatoes. Add the tomatoes,
onion, olives, half the parsley and the salt and pepper. Peel and
halve the eggs and mix into the salad, then add the anchovies.

Mix the oil, lemon juice and garlic together and sprinkle all over
the salad.

For The Tuna

Brush the tuna fish with a little oil and grill or chargrill until
just cooked through.

To Serve

Place each steak on a bed of salad, sprinkle with the remaining
parsley and serve, or chill until needed.

Chef's Note

This recipe is gluten free, wheat free and dairy free.

SEAFOOD HOT POT

SERVES 4

🍷 *Grüner Veltliner*
(Austria)

Method

For The Seafood Hot Pot

Melt the butter in a large pan, add the leeks and gently soften for 5 minutes over a low heat.

Add the garlic and thyme. Stir through until fragrant, then pour in the cream and vegetable stock and simmer for 5 minutes.

Add the baby potatoes and simmer for 10 minutes. Carefully stir in the hake and cook for 3 minutes. Next, stir in the prawns and cook for a further 3 minutes. Finally, remove the kernels from the cobs and add to the pan, along with the mussels and heat through for 2 minutes. Season to taste.

To Serve

Garnish with fennel fronds and chopped chives, and serve with warm, crusty garlic bread.

Ingredients

Seafood Hot Pot

30g butter
6 baby leeks (sliced)
3 garlic cloves (peeled, finely chopped)
4 sprigs thyme
250ml double cream
750ml good quality vegetable stock
100g baby potatoes (cleaned, quartered)
2 x 300g fresh hake portions (cut into small chunks)
300g fresh prawns (cleaned)
500g mussels (cleaned)
2 corn cobs (cooked)
sea salt and freshly ground black pepper (to taste)

Garnish

fennel fronds
chives (chopped)

To Serve

4 slices warm, crusty garlic bread

LEMON POSSET WITH RASPBERRIES & SHORTBREAD BISCUIT

SERVES 8

Sparkling Bugey Cerdon (France)

Ingredients

Lemon Posset

4 lemons (juice and zest of)
850ml double cream
280g caster sugar
1 leaf gelatine (soaked in cold water)

Shortbread Biscuits

450g butter (softened)
225g icing sugar
450g plain flour
225g cornflour
20g caster sugar (for sprinkling)

Garnish

1 punnet raspberries

8 glasses

Method

For The Lemon Posset (Prepare ahead)

Bring the cream, sugar and lemon juice and zest to the boil. Stir in the gelatine, then pour through a fine sieve and divide between 8 glasses or bowls. Allow the lemon possets to set in the fridge overnight.

Chef's Tip
Leave the posset mix to rest overnight.

For The Shortbread Biscuits

Preheat the oven to 160ºC.

Cream the butter and sugar together. Fold in the flours and mix well. Roll the dough into 4 logs, each 5cm long. Wrap the logs in cling film and set in the fridge for at least 2 hours.

Once set, unwrap and slice into 5mm discs. Place the discs on a non-stick baking tray and bake until they turn light brown in colour, for about 8 minutes. Remove from the oven and sprinkle with caster sugar.

To Serve

Serve the chilled lemon possets topped with raspberries and the shortbread biscuits on the side.

058
CHEAL'S OF HENLEY

64 High Street, Henley in Arden, B95 5BX

01564 793 856
www.chealsofhenley.co.uk Twitter: @mattcheal07 @chealshenley

T his small town in Warwickshire dates back to medieval times. Cheal's original structure was built in the 17th Century. It has a multitude of original beams and features with the black and white façade adding to the mile long high street of half timbered residences and medieval landmarks.

Cheal's of Henley opened its doors in October 2015. Chef director Matt Cheal is passionate about his food. He attributes his success to his long liaison with Simpsons Michelin restaurant in Edgbaston. The Cheal family has a long association with the catering industry. With encouragement from their parents, Julie and Tony, they all play a part in the family business.

Matt, a former student of University College Birmingham, proudly boasts a string of accolades including winning the British Culinary Federation Chef of the Year competition in both junior and senior classes, a claim no other chef can make. He has experience working in many prestigious kitchens including that of 'Lettonie' in Bath under Martin Blunos and the infamous Jean-Christophe Ansanay of 'Auberge de Île Barbe' in the culinary capital of Lyon.

Matt's eclectic style of cooking uses French produce, locally sourced and foraged ingredients reflecting the seasons. His modern and classical techniques embrace European influences culminating in a magnificent dining experience.

A restaurant with a history right in the centre of Henley in Arden...

CRISPY DUCK EGG, SMOKED HAM HOCK WITH PEA VELOUTE

SERVES 4

Grüner Veltliner 'Fass 4'
(Austria)

Ingredients

Crispy Duck Eggs

4 duck eggs
3 tbsp white wine vinegar
8 tbsp plain flour
1 hen's egg (beaten)
8 tbsp breadcrumbs
1 litre sunflower oil

Smoked Ham Hock

1kg smoked ham hock
1 carrot (roughly chopped)
1 small onion (roughly chopped)
2 sticks celery (roughly chopped)
8 sprigs thyme
1 bay leaf
1 clove garlic

Pea Velouté

800g frozen garden peas
100g spring onions (washed, sliced)
1 tbsp olive oil
1 litre chicken stock
1 tsp caster sugar
20g butter
salt and pepper

To Serve

100g *blanched* peas
1 punnet pea shoots

Method

For The Crispy Duck Eggs

Crack the duck eggs into a bowl, being careful not to break the yolks. Slip your hand under 1 yolk and lift it out of the bowl leaving the white behind. Gently drop the yolk into a pan of simmering water with the vinegar and repeat quickly with the rest of the eggs.

Allow the eggs to poach gently for 2-3 minutes. They should set around the outside, but be liquid in the centre. Use a slotted spoon to lift them into a bowl of iced water.

Drain the eggs on kitchen paper. Pass each egg yolk through the flour, beaten egg and breadcrumbs. Reserve in the fridge.

Chef's Tip

For a healthier option, serve a poached egg instead of crispy duck eggs.

To Prepare The Ham Hock

Place the hock in a pan of water with the vegetables and bring to the boil. Carefully drain and refresh with cold water. Return the hock and vegetables to the pan with the herbs and garlic, cover with water and bring to the boil. Reduce and simmer for 4 hours, or until the bone slips out of the centre.

To Prepare The Pea Velouté

Wash and drain the peas.

Sauté the spring onions in the olive oil for 3 minutes. Once translucent, add the stock, peas and sugar. Bring rapidly to the boil, then reduce to simmer for 4-5 minutes.

Take the velouté off the heat, blend and pass through a sieve. Just before serving add the butter and season with salt and pepper.

To Serve

Heat the sunflower oil to 180°C.

Remove the eggs from the fridge 20 minutes before cooking. Heat the velouté and the peas. Deep fry the eggs until they are crisp and golden on the outside yet still soft inside, about 2-3 minutes.

Spoon the peas into a serving bowl, place the egg on the top and arrange the ham hock by tearing and placing around the egg. Add some pea shoots. Serve the velouté in a jug and pour at the table.

PORK BELLY, KING PRAWN, BUTTERNUT SQUASH & CAPERS

SERVES 4

*The Crusher Viognier
(California, USA)*

Ingredients

Pork Belly
½ pork belly (1-1½kg in weight)
salt

Butternut Squash
1 small butternut squash
75g butter
50ml double cream
salt (pinch of)

King Prawns
4 large king prawns
2 tbsp plain flour
1 large Maris Piper potato (peeled)
500ml sunflower oil

To Serve
1 tbsp veal stock
12 baby kale leaves
1 tbsp Sosa airbag
24 capers

Method

To Prepare And Cook The Pork Belly (Allow 2 days)

Preheat the oven to 80°C (fan).

Remove the bone using a sharp knife and season both sides of the meat with salt. Vac pack the belly in a bag as tightly as possible.

Cook the belly in the oven on steam for 10 hours or overnight. Remove from the oven and press between 2 chopping boards in the fridge. Allow 8 hours for it to set completely. Once set, portion the belly into 250g rectangular pieces and set aside in the fridge.

> **Chef's Tip**
>
> If you can't steam the pork belly, you could roast it over a tray of water for 1½ hours at 175°C (fan).

To Prepare The Butternut Squash

Peel the squash and scoop out 40 small Parisienne balls. Alternatively, cut the squash into neat cubes. Cook the balls or cubes in salted water until tender, refresh in iced water.

Chop the remaining squash for the purée. Cook in a little butter with a pinch of salt and a splash of water. Cover with a tight fitting lid and cook over a gentle heat. Don't allow the squash to colour. When it's completely tender, remove from the heat and blend in a liquidiser with the cream, then pass through a fine sieve.

For The King Prawns

Shell the prawns and remove the heads; try and keep the tail part intact. Dust with flour.

Peel the potato and 'spaghetti' it using a Japanese mandolin. Wrap the potato strings around the prawn from top to bottom. Leave the prawns in the fridge until ready to serve. Preheat the frying oil to 180°C.

To Serve

Heat and colour the pork belly in a frying pan.

Deep fry the prawns for 3-4 minutes until crispy and golden brown. Deep fry the Sosa airbag until it's light and puffy.

Place a spoon of butternut squash purée on a serving plate and drag. Place the pork belly and a prawn next to it and arrange the Sosa airbag, capers, squash balls and kale over the top. Stir the veal stock into the pork pan juices and drizzle the sauce as pictured.

BAKED EGG CUSTARD TART, STRAWBERRY SORBET & BASIL

SERVES 8-10

Gewurztraminer Hugel 2011, Alsace (France)

Ingredients

Sweet Pastry

225g plain flour
150g unsalted butter
75g icing sugar
2 eggs (1 beaten to glaze)
1 egg yolk

Custard Filling

550ml whipping cream
1 vanilla pod (split)
8 egg yolks
80g caster sugar
nutmeg (freshly grated)

Strawberry Sorbet

75g caster sugar
75ml water
20ml lemon juice
250g strawberry purée

To Serve

100g fresh strawberries (chopped)
strawberry purée (to decorate)
20-30 baby basil leaves

23cm loose bottomed tart case

Method

For The Sweet Pastry

Place the flour, butter and icing sugar in a bowl and rub together with your fingers until you have the texture of fresh breadcrumbs.

Beat together one egg and the egg yolk. Add to the flour mixture, stir to combine, ensuring that it is mixed evenly, but do not overwork the mixture. Wrap in cling film and chill for around 2 hours.

Roll the pastry to 2-3mm thick and line the tart case with it. Allow the excess pastry to hang over the edge to be trimmed later. Chill the pastry for 20 minutes before baking.

Preheat the oven to 175ºC (fan).

Line the tart with baking parchment and baking beans and bake for 15 minutes. Remove the beans and paper and continue cooking until golden brown, about 5 minutes. Trim the pastry, brush with beaten egg and return to the oven for 3-4 minutes. Set aside.

For The Custard Filling

Preheat the oven to 125ºC (fan).

Heat the cream with the vanilla pod while you whisk the egg yolks and sugar. Pour the boiling cream onto the yolks and sugar and whisk. Pass the custard through a fine sieve into a jug. Pour the custard into the cooled pastry case and bake for 15 minutes. When cooked, grate nutmeg over the top. Serve at room temperature.

For The Strawberry Sorbet

Place the sugar, water and lemon juice in a pan and bring to the boil to form a syrup. Chill for 20 minutes. Blend with the strawberry purée, then churn in an ice cream machine for 30 minutes. Store in the freezer.

To Serve

Cut the tart into even size portions and place on the plate. Spoon the chopped strawberries onto the plate. Place some dots of strawberry purée around and add a *quenelle* of sorbet. Arrange the basil over the sorbet.

Chef's Tip

Use a hot knife to cut the tart for perfectly smooth portions.

Cheal's OF HENLEY
01564 793856

THE CHERRY HOUSE AT WERRINGTON

125 Church Street, Werrington, Peterborough, PE4 6QF

01733 571 721
www.cherryhouserestaurant.co.uk Twitter: @cherryhouse125

There are few restaurants that can boast two decades of continuous ownership, but The Cherry House at Werrington is unique in many ways.

Under the control of chef patron Andrew Corrick, formerly head chef at The Park Lane Hotel in Mayfair, the restaurant offers visitors fine British dining with a respectful nod to classic French in a 400 year old quintessential English country cottage, built using local stone. Located just three and a half miles from the hubbub of the city centre, thankfully The Cherry House in its village setting, feels a million miles away.

History has the building used by Oliver Cromwell as he plotted the King's downfall; the name itself derives from the original Cherry House which formed part of Cherry Farm, well known for its 'Werrington Cherries'. The kitchen today continues to utilise locally produced ingredients and ethically sourced fish. An ever-evolving menu, the table d'hote changes fortnightly and the Sunday lunch menu is refreshed monthly.

The Cherry House at Werrington offers something for the serious food lovers, for those romantic evenings, corporate entertaining and for those just enjoying fine, fresh food prepared with care and attention to detail. With emphasis on traditional hospitality, excellent service and a relaxed, friendly atmosphere, The Cherry House at Werrington is certainly looking forward not back.

Working under chef patron Andrew Corrick is head chef David Marshall, who has been at The Cherry House since 2002. Andrew and David are supported by a highly enthusiastic team, proud of some excellent reviews in the Eastern England media and the online world.

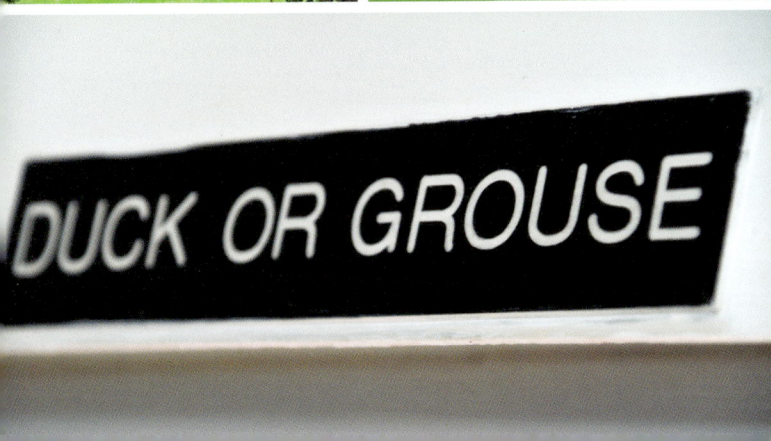

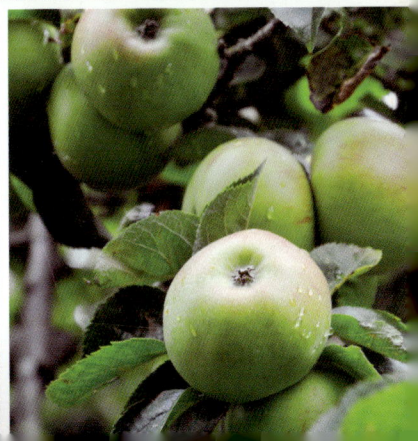

DUCK OR GROUSE

SAUTEED KING PRAWNS IN PROSCIUTTO, ASPARAGUS, TOMATO SALSA

SERVES 4

Picpoul de Pinet 'Les Prades', Caves de l'Ormarine (France)

Ingredients

King Prawns

16 king prawns (peeled, cleaned)
8 slices prosciutto
butter (knob of)
olive oil (for frying)
seasoning

Tomato Salsa

4 vine plum tomatoes
1 tbsp brown sugar
2 tbsp white wine vinegar
250ml dry white wine
1 clove garlic (crushed)
150ml extra virgin olive oil
8 leaves basil (*chiffonade*)
seasoning

Asparagus

16 asparagus spears
butter (knob of)
seasoning

Garnish

8 small heads basil
balsamic syrup (drizzle of)

Method

For The Tomato Salsa

Blanch, peel and deseed the vine tomatoes and cut into *concasse*.

Place the sugar into a small pan with a little water and caramelise. When caramelised, add the white wine vinegar and reduce by two thirds. Stir in the white wine and garlic and reduce by half, then add the chopped tomatoes, olive oil and basil leaves. Season to taste.

For The King Prawns

Cut the prosciutto in half lengthways. Season the prawns and wrap in prosciutto. Colour in a hot frying pan with a little butter and olive oil, then turn over.

For The Asparagus

Cut the asparagus spears to about 10cm long and peel the ends. *Blanch* lightly in boiling, salted water. Toss the asparagus in a knob of butter and season.

To Serve

Place the heated asparagus on a plate, sit the prawns on top, dress with a little salsa on either side and drizzle with balsamic syrup. Finish with the basil heads.

> **Chef's Tip**
>
> The freshness of ingredients is paramount and will make all the difference to the dish.

FILLET OF GRASMERE FARM PORK WITH SAGE, PARSNIP MASH, RICH CALVADOS JUS

SERVES 4

Grayson Cellars Zinfandel
(California, USA)

Ingredients

Fillet Of Pork

4 x 150g centre cut pork fillets (fully trimmed)
16 leaves sage (finely chopped)
seasoning
25ml olive oil
10g butter

Parsnip Crisps

1 medium parsnip (peeled)
vegetable oil (for frying)
salt

Calvados Jus

1 banana shallot (finely chopped)
8 leaves sage (finely chopped)
1 clove garlic (crushed)
25ml calvados
275ml dry cider
1½ litres veal stock
50g unsalted butter
seasoning

Parsnip Mash

1kg medium sized parsnips (peeled, cored)
60g butter
50ml double cream
seasoning

To Serve

12 baby carrots (peeled, trimmed, cooked al dente)
12 asparagus tips (*blanched*)
20g butter
seasoning

Garnish

¼ punnet amaranth micro cress

Method

For The Fillet Of Pork

Season the pork fillet and roll in chopped sage. Wrap tightly in cling film and refrigerate.

> **Chef's Tip**
>
> It is best to roll the pork fillets in the sage and refrigerate overnight.

For The Parsnip Crisps

Slice the parsnip on a mandolin, then dry on a clean tea towel.

Heat the vegetable oil to 180°C and deep fry the parsnip slices for 2-3 minutes until coloured.

Remove and place on kitchen paper. Season with salt.

For The Calvados Jus

Sauté the shallot, sage and garlic in half the butter for 3-4 minutes over a medium heat.

Flambé with calvados, then add the cider, reducing to a glaze. Stir in the stock and reduce to a third. Season, sieve and set aside.

For The Parsnip Mash

Place the parsnips in salted water and bring to the boil, then reduce to a simmer.

When cooked, remove from heat and drain. Return to the pan and place on a low heat to evaporate any moisture. Mash to a smooth consistency, add the butter, cream and seasoning. Keep warm.

For The Fillet Of Pork

Preheat the oven to 200°C.

Place a frying pan over a medium heat, then add the butter and olive oil.

Remove the fillet from the cling film and place in the pan, turning for an even, light colour. Transfer to the oven for 10-12 minutes until cooked. Rest for 2 minutes.

To Serve

Add the carrots and asparagus to a pan with the butter and season. Plate the parsnip mash, slice the pork fillet and place on top. Arrange the asparagus, carrots and crisps as pictured. Reheat the jus, then whisk in the remaining butter, check the seasoning and dress on the side of the pork. Sprinkle with amaranth micro cress.

MR GIBBONS' STICKY TOFFEE PUDDING, BUTTERSCOTCH SAUCE, VANILLA ICE CREAM

SERVES 8-10

🍷 *Late Harvest Sauvignon Blanc, Viña Morandé (Chile)*

Ingredients

Sticky Toffee Pudding

75g butter (soft)
175g dark muscovado sugar
1½ tbsp golden syrup
1½ tbsp black treacle
2 eggs
1 tsp vanilla extract
200g self-raising flour (plus extra for dusting)
200g dried dates (pitted)
300ml water
2 tsp bicarbonate of soda

Butterscotch Sauce

125g butter
125g dark muscovado sugar
250ml double cream

Vanilla Ice Cream

1 plump vanilla pod (split lengthways, scraped)
300ml full-fat milk
300ml double cream
100g caster sugar
4 egg yolks

Garnish

mint sprigs
icing sugar (to dust)

8-10 mini loaf tins

Method

For The Sticky Toffee Pudding

Preheat oven to 180°C.

Grease the loaf tins using one third of the butter, then dust with flour.

Blend the remaining butter and sugar in a mixer.

Mix the syrup, treacle, eggs and vanilla extract in a bowl. Slowly add to the butter and sugar and continue to mix. Turn the mixer to low, add the flour and mix evenly.

Place the dates in a saucepan with the water and bring to the boil. Remove from heat and liquidise.

While still hot, mix in the bicarbonate of soda. Fold the dates into the egg mixture, then place into the tins to two-thirds full.

Bake for 30 minutes. Remove from the oven and cool for 10 minutes. Loosen with a knife, turn upside down and tap the puddings out.

For The Butterscotch Sauce

Melt the butter and sugar in a pan and mix well. Add the cream, bring to the boil and simmer until thickened slightly.

For The Vanilla Ice Cream (Prepare ahead)

Place the vanilla pod and seeds in a pan with the milk and cream. Bring to the boil, remove from the heat and leave to infuse.

Mix the sugar and egg yolks in a bowl and whisk until pale and fluffy. Put the vanilla cream back on the heat and bring to almost boiling point. Pour onto the egg mix, whisking all the time.

Return to the heat and whisk until it begins to thicken. Sieve into a bowl and allow to cool. Churn in an ice cream machine.

To Serve

Place the warm pudding in a bowl with the sauce and a ball of ice cream on top, decorating with a vanilla pod and a sprig of mint. Dust with icing sugar.

Chef's Tip

This dessert can be made in advance and reheated without detriment. Simply reheat the puddings in the microwave and warm the sauce over a gentle heat.

THE CROSS AT KENILWORTH

16 New Street, Kenilworth, CV8 2EZ

01926 853 840
www.thecrosskenilworth.co.uk Twitter: @TheCrossKen

Diners at The Cross at Kenilworth enjoy the relaxed setting of a popular village pub but with the culinary finesse of a Michelin starred and professionally trained chef, Adam Bennett.

The pub was taken over by celebrated Midland's restaurateur Andreas Antona in the summer of 2013. A major refurbishment followed which restored some of the 19th Century inn's original features and created a relaxing and stylish dining space.

Within one year of its reopening, the team at The Cross had secured a Michelin star, one of only 14 awarded to new restaurants in 2014.

Prior to taking over the kitchen at The Cross, chef director Adam Bennett spent 10 years working for Andreas at Simpsons in Edgbaston, having previously worked in London's top kitchens. He is passionate about food and takes inspiration from many sources.

At The Cross, locals can enjoy drinks and light snacks in the bar or in the garden during the warmer months. Those seeking something more substantial won't ever be disappointed; Adam's talent for creating simple, perfectly balanced dishes produces a regularly changing menu using the very best seasonal ingredients.

As well as the garden, set lunch and à la carte menus, The Cross also offers a five course tasting menu which Adam has put together to include his most popular signature dishes. Giuseppe Longobardi, a judge at the Sommelier Wine Awards, manages the restaurant.

The Cross is owned by celebrated Midland's chef turned restaurateur, Andreas Antona and headed up by chef director, Adam Bennett. Adam has twice represented the UK and achieved the best result to date for a UK chef in the Bocuse d'Or.

MELON, FETA, BASIL, POMEGRANATE, SALTED MELON SEEDS

SERVES 4

🍷 *Vermentino Di Sardegna 'I Fiori' Pala Sardegna, (Italy)*

Ingredients

1 ripe Charentais melon
½ ripe Galia melon
400g wedge watermelon
½ ripe pomegranate

Salted Melon Seeds

25g melon seeds (peeled)
10g caster sugar
3g salt
chilli powder (pinch of)
15ml olive oil

Basil Oil

100ml grapeseed oil
50g basil leaves
fine salt (pinch of)

To Serve

150g feta cheese (cubed)
40 small basil leaves
balsamic vinegar
Maldon salt flakes

Method

For The Melon And Pomegranate

Peel and deseed the melons, reserving the seeds. Cut the Charentais and Galia into slices. The watermelon should be cut into 1cm cubes.

Remove the seeds from the pomegranate and reserve with the melon in the fridge.

Chef's Tip

If you are lucky enough to have a vacuum pack machine, then pack the prepared melons on full pressure for one hour before serving. This will bring out the sweetness of the melon.

For The Salted Melon Seeds

Combine the seeds, sugar, salt and olive oil in a shallow pan and cook over a moderate heat, stirring constantly. When the seeds are a pale golden colour, add a pinch of chilli powder and drain immediately on kitchen towel. Store in an airtight container when cool.

For The Basil Oil

Process the oil, basil and salt briefly in a liquidiser.

Heat the mixture quickly to 104°C in a pan, using a probe thermometer to check the temperature.

Tip the mixture into a metal bowl set over ice to chill rapidly.

Strain the oil through muslin or cheese cloth. Reserve the oil and discard the solids.

To Serve

Arrange the melon slices and cubes on each plate, add the feta cubes and pomegranate seeds.

Sprinkle with a few melon seeds and basil leaves. Finish with the basil oil, balsamic vinegar and a few flakes of Maldon salt.

COD, FRESH WHITE BEANS, CHORIZO, PEPPERS, BASIL

SERVES 4

Torrontés, Terrazas Mendoza (Argentina)

Ingredients

4 x 125g cod fillets
4 tbsp Maldon salt crystals

Beans

200g fresh coco rubico beans (podded)
1 litre vegetable stock
2 sprigs thyme
1 bay leaf
10 white peppercorns (cracked)
2 cloves garlic (cracked)

Peppers

2 red peppers
2 yellow peppers
1 shallot (chopped)
1 clove garlic
50ml olive oil
salt (pinch of)

To Finish The Beans

50ml olive oil
50g chorizo (finely diced)
125g reserved bean stock
saffron filaments (pinch of)
Espelette pepper powder (pinch of)
smoked paprika (pinch of)
125g unsalted butter
1 tsp lemon juice
salt (pinch of)
basil (handful of, chopped)

To Serve

basil oil
250g washed leaf spinach
50g butter

Method

For The Cod

Coat each portion of cod lightly with Maldon salt. Refrigerate for 20 minutes, then rinse in cold water. Dry well and reserve in the fridge.

> **Chef's Tip**
>
> Salting the cod before cooking will firm the fish to give a lovely flaking texture.

To Cook The Beans

Bring the beans and vegetable stock to the boil, then reduce to a bare simmer. Skim, then add the other ingredients tied in a muslin bag.

Cook until tender, about 40 minutes. Remove from the heat, add a little salt and reserve.

For The Peppers

Brush the peppers with olive oil and grill to blister the skins. Peel and dice the pepper flesh.

Cook the shallot and garlic in the remaining olive oil until soft.

Add the peppers and a pinch of salt, cook gently until they are soft and sweet. Reserve until needed.

To Finish The Beans

Gently cook the chorizo in the olive oil for 3-4 minutes. Add the reserved bean stock, saffron, Espelette and smoked paprika. Simmer for 3-4 minutes.

Whisk in the butter, then add the drained beans and heat through gently. Add salt if needed and the lemon juice. Stir through the basil and peppers just before serving.

To Cook The Fish And Serve

Preheat the oven to 80°C (fan).

Brush the fish with olive oil and cook in the oven for 10-14 minutes, or until the flakes separate when pressed and the fish is still moist. Brush with basil oil.

Wilt the spinach in butter, season, drain and place a little at the centre of each plate. Spoon the beans around and place the fish on top.

CHOCOLATE & CHESTNUT TART, COCOA BEAN ICE CREAM

SERVES 8

Maury Rouge Domaine Mas Amiel Vin Doux Naturel (France)

Ingredients

Chocolate Pastry Case

125g unsalted butter (chilled, diced)
125g plain flour
4g cocoa powder
salt (pinch of)
25g egg yolk
50g caster sugar

Chestnut Mi-Cuit Mixture

90g Jivara 40% milk chocolate
90g unsalted butter
90g egg
60g sugar
15g honey
15g plain flour
15g potato starch
salt (pinch of)
200g candied chestnuts (chopped, reserve 4 for decoration)

Piping Ganache

300ml whipping cream
30g honey
306g Valrhona Caraibe 60% chocolate (melted)
20g unsalted butter

Cocoa Bean Ice Cream

500ml full-fat milk
5 egg yolks
75g sugar
50g cocoa nibs (lightly toasted)

28cm loose bottomed tart tin

Method

Chef's Tip

Make all of the components of the tart one day before to spread the work.

For The Chocolate Pastry Case

Sift the cocoa, flour and salt together. Rub the butter into the flour mixture.

Whisk the egg yolk with the sugar. Combine the yolk and sugar mixture with the flour and butter until smooth. Wrap in cling film and chill for 1 hour or until set.

Preheat the oven to 165°C (fan).

Roll the pastry out to 3mm thickness. Line the case and bake blind for 15-20 minutes, remove the beans and bake for a further 5-10 minutes until crisp. Leave to cool.

For The Chestnut Mi-Cuit Mixture

Preheat the oven to 165°C (fan).

Melt the chocolate and butter together. Add the egg, honey and sugar and mix well. Stir in the flour, potato starch and salt.

Spread a 1cm layer in the bottom of the baked tart case. Sprinkle with the chopped chestnuts and bake for 8 minutes. Remove from the oven and leave to cool.

For The Piping Ganache

Bring the cream and honey to the boil, then cool to 40°C. Combine with the chocolate to give a smooth *emulsion*.

Add the butter and chill the mixture in a piping bag for 3 hours, or overnight. Pipe the ganache in a spiral over the cooled tart.

For The Cocoa Bean Ice Cream

Bring the milk to the boil. Whisk the yolks and sugar together, then whisk in the hot milk. Return to the pan and stir over a low heat until slightly thickened (about 84°C).

Cool immediately and churn in an ice cream machine. Lightly crush the cocoa nibs and combine with the churned ice cream. Reserve in the freezer.

To Finish And Serve

Use a warm knife to cut wedges from the tart. Serve with the cocoa bean ice cream, half a candied chestnut and decorate as you wish.

088
EL BORRACHO DE ORO

Harborne Court, Harborne Road, Edgbaston, Birmingham, B15 3BU

0121 454 5368

www.elborracho.co.uk Twitter: @ElBorrachoDeOro Facebook: El Borracho de Oro

Authentic tapas in a family friendly environment has caused a stir on Birmingham's vibrant gastronomic scene. The city, which now boasts five Michelin stars, has become enthralled by the recently opened El Borracho De Oro.

The tapas bar, in salubrious Edgbaston, is the brainchild of accomplished restaurateur Emma Yufera-Ruiz, who has successfully opened and run three tapas bars in Shropshire and the West Midlands.

The dream was to provide the best in food and hospitality on the outskirts of the city centre and El Borracho De Oro has helped achieve that.

The large, open plan restaurant boasts a passionate and enthusiastic kitchen and front of house team that is committed to making El Borracho De Oro one of the best Spanish restaurants in the UK.

Beautiful ceramics, plush golden upholstery, brooding red walls and colourful, glass lights give the restaurant atmosphere and class, while the unfussy food and service creates a 'home from home' ambience.

An impressive selection of wine, beer and cider, all authentically Spanish, features the best of España; with the 60-bin wine list a particular highlight.

The freshest and tastiest ingredients bring the Mediterranean to the heart of Brum. Exceptional quality features on an innovative and creative menu, with grilled Iberico pork steak paired with cheese sauce, fried squid partnered with squid ink aioli and piquillo peppers stuffed with Spanish black pudding.

"We're passionate about what we do. From the food to the tables, the beautiful ceramics to the lighting; we're committed to bringing Spanish sunshine to England's second city", says Emma.

¡Y Viva España!

The team is full of passion and enthusiasm to be one of the best Spanish restaurants in the UK.

CREAMY BLACK TIGER KING PRAWN RICE

SERVES 4

Val De Monxes, Albariño (Spain)
*Fresh, smooth and lively, very pale straw with gold
tones. Intense mature fruits on the nose.*

Ingredients

8 big, black tiger prawns

Creamy Rice

320g bomba rice (paella rice)
1 litre concentrated prawn stock
250g black tiger king prawn meat
100ml olive oil
1 medium onion (chopped)
1 clove garlic (chopped)
½ tsp sweet paprika
½ tin top quality chopped tomatoes

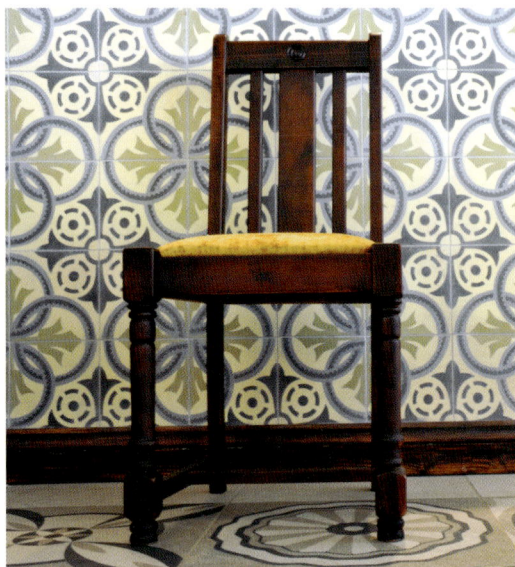

Method

For The Creamy Rice

Gently shallow fry the onions in olive oil until transparent, then
add the garlic and paprika. Stir briefly, then add the tomatoes.
Continue to cook over a gentle heat to create a shiny 'sofrito'.
Add the rice and pour in half of the stock, stirring well.

Keep stirring, as you would with a risotto, until all the stock
has been absorbed, adding more stock until the rice is cooked to
your liking (al dente is our preferred way). Season to taste.

For The Prawns

Grill the tiger prawns in a hot pan.

To Serve

Top the rice with the prawns and serve.

> **Chef's Tip**
>
> The key to this dish is making a fantastic prawn or seafood
> stock, full of flavour and concentrated.

PORK CHEEKS IN RED WINE SAUCE

SERVES 6

Tempranillo, Pesquera Crianza, Ribera del Duero,
Bodegas Alejandro Fernández (Spain)

Ingredients

Pork Cheeks

6 pork cheeks
50g wheatflour
250ml extra virgin olive oil
2 medium onions (*julienne*)
1 leek (*julienne*)
3 carrots (*julienne*)
350ml good red wine (Rioja or Ribera)
4 cloves garlic
5g salt

Catalan Spinach Salad

50g baby spinach leaves (washed)
30g mixed salad leaves
15g raisins
15g pine nuts (toasted)
¼ orange (peeled, seeded, cut into small pieces)
salt and pepper (to season)

Salad Dressing

30ml olive oil
5ml dark honey
5ml sherry vinegar

To Serve

olive oil mashed potato or fondant potatoes

Method

For The Pork Cheeks

Lightly flour the pork cheeks.

Heat the olive oil in a stew pot over a medium-high heat. Brown the cheeks until completely seared to prevent any loss of meat juices. Remove the pork cheeks from the pot and place them on a plate to rest.

Poach the vegetables in the same oil until they are golden brown - stirring occasionally to prevent them from burning. Add the red wine and reduce until all the alcohol has evaporated. Add the garlic, return the pork cheeks to the pan and cover with water. Simmer on a low heat for 2 hours, adding more water if necessary.

Remove the pork cheeks once cooked. Using a blender, purée the vegetables and liquid to make a rich sauce. Pass the sauce through a *chinois* to get a smooth and elegant sauce.

For The Catalan Spinach Salad

Simply mix all the ingredients together, making sure that you season the salad well. Do not squash or crush the leaves too much. Drizzle with the salad dressing and serve immediately. Enjoy whilst it is still crisp and fresh.

To Serve

Serve the pork cheeks with the sauce and perhaps the Catalan spinach salad on the side, or with some olive oil mashed potato or fondant potatoes.

CREMA CATALANA INFUSIONADA CON CITRICOS
(SPANISH CREME BRULEE INFUSED WITH CITRUS FRUITS)

SERVES 6

🍷 *Don PX (Pedro Ximénez) Vino Dulce (sweet wine)*
(Málaga, Spain)
*The 1976 Don PX Reserva Especial vintage from
Bodegas Toro Albala has been declared as a
special secret by the family owners. Very small
production and only a few bottles remain, the
family consider this vintage one of their best!*

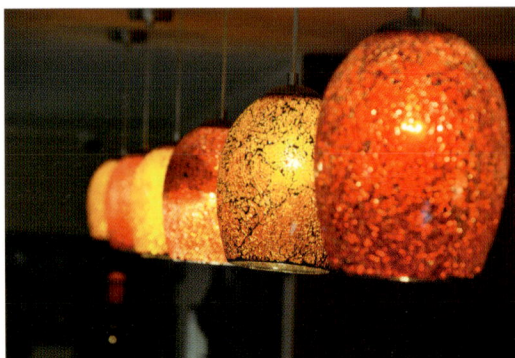

Ingredients

Crema Catalana

190ml full-fat milk
600ml double cream
½ orange (peel of)
½ lemon (peel of)
1 vanilla pod
1 single measure triple sec (or other
orange-based liqueur)
125g sugar
8 egg yolks

To Serve

caster sugar (to sprinkle)
candied peel

6 ramekins or small earthenware dishes

Method

For The Crema Catalana

Preheat the oven to 95°C.

Place the ramekins into a deep roasting tin.

On a low heat in a large pan, add the milk, cream, orange and
lemon peels, vanilla and triple sec. Once the cream and milk
mixture starts to bubble, remove it from the heat and leave to
infuse for 5-10 minutes.

Strain the mixture making sure you retain all the liquid.

Mix the sugar and egg yolks together. Use a little of the warm
milk to mix into the egg yolks, making sure you whisk all the
time, until well incorporated. Add the yolks into the original milk
pan along with the rest of the milk mixture and very, very gently
heat, stirring all the time. After about 10 minutes it should
thicken slightly, until it coats the back of a spoon.

Transfer the thin custard into the ramekins. Pour water into the
roasting tin to come half way up the sides, making a *bain-marie*.

Place in the oven for 1 hour, turning the heat up to 110°C for
the last 10 minutes. This should result in a set but perfectly
creamy Crema Catalana. Remove from the oven and allow to
cool completely.

To Serve

Sprinkle plenty of caster sugar on top of the set cream and
burn with a kitchen blowtorch or under the grill. The sugar will
burn and go a brown, caramel colour, creating a crunchy crust.

098
FAIRLAWNS RESTAURANT

Little Aston Road, Aldridge, Walsall, WS9 0NU

01922 455 122
www.fairlawns.co.uk Twitter: @fairlawnshotel

The team at Fairlawns make guests feel welcome as soon as they step through the doors. The aim is to create a relaxed, attentive and comfortable service, so visitors can enjoy special occasions together.

The food produced at Fairlawns is essentially British - building upon classic foundations and taking influences from popular flavours in British cuisine. Special dishes twist traditional everyday flavour combinations, and signature meals rely on showcasing their quality ingredients, by serving them simply, so that the flavours speak for themselves. All food is freshly prepared with care, showing respect for seasonality.

Both classic and modern wines are carefully selected to complement the food in the restaurant. Guests are offered a carefully balanced choice of style, grape variety, country of origin and price, all from successful vintages, many of which have won major awards.

As well as the restaurant, Fairlawns offer private dining and can cater for intimate dinner parties or banquets. They have been awarded 2 AA Rosettes for fine cuisine and their objective is to maintain these accolades and, maybe one day, be awarded three.

Naturally, Fairlawns endeavours to keep up with food trends but they also consider it important to offer food which is simple, has not been over prepared and celebrates the ingredients. As we all know, this is sometimes when food is at its best. They pride themselves on maintaining traditional standards, offering warm hospitality (with a sense of humour) and giving the guests an environment in which to relax and enjoy.

Family run for 30 years and a holder of
2 Rosettes for most of those.
At Fairlawns, food and hospitality comes
from the heart.

HAM HOCK TERRINE

SERVES 4

Crystallum, Clay Shales Chardonnay, 2009
(South Africa)
Excellent vintage; crisp apples, creamy hazelnut
and delicious minerality to cleanse the palate.

Ingredients

2 large ham hocks (rinsed for 5 minutes)

Pickled Eggs

8 quail eggs
100ml white wine vinegar
50ml white wine
1 tsp salt, 6 black peppercorns
2 tsp honey, 50ml water

Stock

1 carrot, 1 leek, 2 sticks celery
thyme (bunch of)
1 large white onion
4 black peppercorns
2 bay leaves, 3 litres cold water

Stock Reduction

100ml cooking liquid (stock)
250ml cider
1½ sheets gelatine (soaked in cold water)
3 tsp wholegrain mustard
3 tsp parsley (chopped)

Pickle

80g carrot
50g golden beetroot
2 cloves garlic, 20g dried apricot
20g dried dates, 25g raisins
80g cauliflower, 80g onion (diced)
60g apple (diced), 25g gherkin (diced)
80g dark brown sugar
20ml lemon juice, 200ml malt vinegar
1 tsp Worcester sauce
½ tsp ground cumin, ½ tsp allspice
½ tsp black pepper, 2 tsp arrowroot

Garnish

micro herbs, carrot curls (raw)
cauliflower florets (raw)

terrine mould

Method

For The Pickled Eggs (Allow 3 days)

Boil the eggs for 2½ minutes, then chill. Bring the remaining ingredients to the boil, then simmer for 3 minutes. Chill. Peel the quail eggs and add to the pickling liquor. Leave for 2-3 days in the fridge.

For The Ham Hock And Stock (Prepare the day before)

Add all the stock ingredients and the hocks to a large pan and bring to the boil. Simmer until the ham is tender, approximately 2½ hours, skimming the scum regularly. When cool enough to handle, remove the meat from the bones.

For The Stock Reduction

In a separate pan, reduce 100ml of stock and add the gelatine to melt it. Stir in the mustard, parsley and cider.

To Assemble The Ham Hock Terrine

Combine the picked meat with the stock reduction and mix well. Place into a terrine mould lined with cling film and leave to set in the fridge overnight.

To Make The Pickle (Prepare the day before)

Dice the vegetables into ½cm squares. Combine all the ingredients, except the arrowroot, in a pan and simmer for 1½ hours. Stir in the arrowroot and cook until thickened. Refrigerate overnight.

To Serve

Assemble the dish as in the photograph.

Chef's Tips

Ensure you wash the ham hocks thoroughly. Retain the flavour of the eggs by keeping the pickle spices to a minimum.

DUO OF LAMB

SERVES 4

Rioja, Viña Ardanza Reserva Especial, La Rioja Alta 2005 (Spain)
Excellent supplier, wonderful vintage.

Ingredients

Mint Jelly

½ bunch mint
50ml water
100ml white wine vinegar
100g caster sugar
2g agar agar

Lamb Shoulder

500g piece lamb shoulder
300ml red wine
1 litre lamb stock
3 banana shallots (finely diced)
50g butter
50g capers
100ml sherry vinegar
100ml cooking liquor
salt
flour, beaten eggs, panko breadcrumbs (to *pane*)

Fondant Potatoes

4 medium Maris Piper potatoes
150g butter
100ml chicken stock
thyme (sprig of)
2 cloves garlic

Lamb Rack

2 x 4 bone lamb racks
butter (knob of)

Pea Purée

150g frozen peas
100ml vegetable stock
salt and pepper

Garnish

40 broad beans
8 sprigs purple sprouting broccoli
watercress

Method

For The Mint Jelly

Pick the mint leaves. Bring the water, sugar and white wine vinegar to the boil. Add the mint and steep for 4 minutes. Blitz in food processor and pass through a sieve. Bring back to the boil, then whisk in the agar agar. Chill in the fridge to set.

For The Lamb Shoulder (Prepare the day before)

Preheat the oven to 120°C (fan).

Braise the shoulder in red wine and stock for 3 hours. Allow to cool, then shred.

Sweat the shallots in butter until transparent, add the capers and *deglaze* the pan with sherry vinegar and the remaining lamb cooking liquor. Mix this into the shredded shoulder and season. Wrap in cling film and roll into a cylinder. Chill overnight.

For The Fondant Potatoes

Cut the potatoes into fondant shape. Melt the butter in a pan, then add potatoes. Keep cooking in the butter, turning regularly, until the butter foams. When the potatoes start to brown, add the stock, garlic and thyme. Cover the pan and simmer gently until cooked, about 25 minutes.

For The Rack Of Lamb

Preheat the oven to 180°C (fan).

Colour the lamb in a hot pan with butter. Season and roast the racks of lamb for 14 minutes. Leave to rest.

> **Chef's Tip**
> Ensure you colour and season the fat to enhance the flavour.

For The Pea Purée

Bring the vegetable stock to the boil. Add the peas and cook on a rolling boil for 3 minutes. Season, then blend in a food processor. Pass through a sieve. Keep on a low heat.

For The Garnish

Pod the broad beans and *blanch* in salted water for 2 minutes. Trim the broccoli florets and *blanch* in salted water for 2 minutes.

To Serve

Preheat the oven to 180°C (fan).

Remove the cling film from the lamb shoulder. Roll in flour, beaten egg, then breadcrumbs. Cut into slices, sauté in hot butter, then roast in the oven for 12 minutes. Assemble the dish as pictured.

STRAWBERRY CHEESECAKE

SERVES 4

🍷 *Champagne, Etienne Lefèvre, Grand Cru (France)*
Our house Champagne from an eight hectare
estate. Finish your meal in style!

Ingredients

Cheesecake

125ml milk
1 tsp vanilla extract
50g caster sugar
2 leaves gelatine (soaked in cold water)
40g egg yolk
150g cream cheese
165ml double cream

Strawberry Jelly

100g strawberry purée
30g caster sugar
1.2g agar agar

Strawberry Gel

100g strawberry purée
20g sugar
1g agar agar
0.3g xanthan gum

Pistachio Meringue

1 egg white
60g caster sugar
5g roasted pistachios

Coconut Tuile

25g desiccated coconut
25g icing sugar
½ egg (beaten)
10g unsalted butter

Cardamom Ice Cream

4 egg yolks
400ml double cream, 200ml full-fat milk
200g caster sugar
4 roasted cardamom pods

Garnish

baby strawberries, micro basil leaves
strawberry jelly cubes

4 x 5cm ring moulds

Method

For The Cheesecake

Bring the milk, sugar and vanilla to the boil. Add the yolks and cook until the mixture coats the back of a spoon. Remove from the heat and add the gelatine to the mixture while it is warm. Whip the double cream and beat the cream cheese until soft. Combine all the ingredients until fully incorporated and set in 5cm moulds in the fridge for a minimum of 4 hours.

For The Strawberry Jelly

Bring the purée to the boil, add the sugar and stir until dissolved. Add the agar agar, pour out to a thin layer onto a flat tray and leave to set.

For The Gel

Bring the purée to a light boil, add the sugar and when dissolved, add the agar agar. Set aside to cool, then add the xanthan gum. Chill in the fridge, then blitz to a purée when cold.

For The Pistachio Meringue

Preheat the oven to 115°C (fan).

Whisk the egg white with half the sugar on full speed until soft peaks form, then add the remaining sugar and incorporate. Spread thinly onto a baking mat on a non-stick tray and sprinkle with the chopped pistachios.

Bake for 1 hour. Break into shards and store in an airtight container.

For The Coconut Tuile

Preheat the oven to 140°C (fan).

Cream all the ingredients together. Spread thinly onto a tray and bake until golden brown, about 5-8 minutes. Cut to shape whilst hot.

For The Cardamom Ice Cream

Heat the milk, cardamom and cream to 90°C, then stir in the egg yolks and sugar. Bring back to 82°C, remove from the heat, and allow to cool. When cold, blitz the mix, then freeze in a lidded container.

To Serve

Carefully roll the cheesecakes in the jelly in the tray and cut to fit. Swipe the gel in the centre of the plate. Add all the elements as shown, finishing with a *quenelle* of ice cream.

> **Chef's Tip**
>
> Take the cheesecake out of the fridge 10 minutes before serving. You can prepare all elements of this dish in advance.

108
FISHMORE HALL

Fishmore Road, Ludlow, Shropshire, SY8 3DP

01584 875 148
www.fishmorehall.co.uk Twitter: @fishmorehall

Dating from the late 1800s, Fishmore Hall was originally a family home, but when the Penman family arrived, the once magnificent Georgian house had become semi derelict after years of neglect. Reopening in 2007 as a hotel and restaurant following extensive renovations, Fishmore Hall has developed a reputation as one of the UK's up-and-coming venues for fine dining, as well as a great place to stay in comfort and contemporary style. Awarded 2 AA Rosettes within weeks of opening, the restaurant, renamed Forelles following the addition of a new orangery extension, earned its third Rosette and the hotel's three red stars in 2011, recognising it as one of the top 200 'Inspectors' Choice' establishments in the whole of the UK.

Located on the outskirts of Ludlow, a mecca for food lovers, and in the midst of the beautiful rolling south Shropshire countryside, it's hardly surprising that head chef Andrew Birch sources almost everything (except the seafood, of course) from the surrounding area, ensuring the highest quality and freshest ingredients.

With its 15 individually styled bedrooms and designer bathrooms, this is just the place for a romantic weekend getaway or special celebration. It has also become increasingly popular as a perfect venue for weddings and other family gatherings, as well as being ideally placed for out-of-town business meetings and seminars.

Set on a hillside overlooking the historic town of Ludlow, Fishmore Hall is delighting its guests with fantastic food that has earned its restaurant, Forelles, 3 AA Rosettes. The hotel has also been recognised as an AA Inspectors' Choice.

CAULIFLOWER, TUNWORTH, CAPER, SOURDOUGH CROUTONS

SERVES 4

🍷 *Sauvignon Blanc, Buitenverwachting, 2014 (South Africa)*

Ingredients

Roasted Cauliflower

1 cauliflower
10g butter (melted)

Cheese Sauce

30g Tunworth cheese (finely grated, plus a little extra to garnish)
30g Gruyère cheese (finely grated)
100ml double cream
5ml white wine

Caper And Golden Raisin Purée

100g capers (plus extra to garnish)
100g golden raisins

Chive Oil

100g fresh chives
100ml olive oil

Garnish

1 loaf sourdough bread (thinly sliced, toasted until crisp)
fresh truffle
salt and pepper (to season)

Method

For The Roasted Cauliflower

Break the cauliflower into nice size florets, add the melted butter, salt and pepper and cook in a waterbath at 85°C for 25 minutes. Once cooked, refresh in iced water and set aside. Alternatively, *blanch* the cauliflower in salted, boiling water until tender and refresh in iced water.

For The Cheese Sauce

Boil the cream, season and add the white wine. Stir in the grated cheese until melted, pass through a fine sieve and set aside.

For The Caper And Golden Raisin Purée

Place the capers and golden raisins in a pan, cover with water and simmer for 1 hour. Blend until smooth, pass through a sieve, and chill.

For The Chive Oil

Blend the chives and oil together to give you a vibrant, green oil, then pass through a sieve.

To Serve

Roast the cauliflower evenly until golden brown. Put a spoonful of the cheese sauce in the serving dish, place the roasted cauliflower on top, sprinkle over some capers and some pieces of sourdough croûtes. Place some dots of purée on the cauliflower, finish with the chive oil and a little freshly grated truffle.

Chef's Tip

When possible, use fresh Wiltshire truffle.

LINE CAUGHT TURBOT, BACON, ONION, CEPS, WILD GARLIC, MUSTARD SAUCE

SERVES 4

Gavi di Gavi, La Meirana, 2013 (Italy)

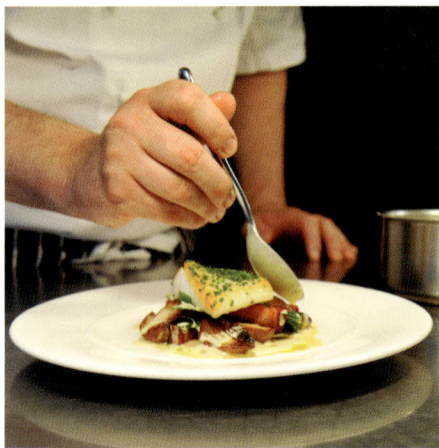

Ingredients

4 x 175g pieces turbot

Mustard Sauce

100ml white wine
100ml chicken stock
100ml veal stock
500ml double cream
10g Dijon mustard
20g English mustard

Braised Baby Onions

8 baby onions (peeled)
salt and pepper

Garnish

50g smoked belly bacon lardons
8 ceps
wild garlic (handful of)
chives (chopped)
salt and pepper

Method

For The Mustard Sauce

Reduce the white wine, chicken stock and veal stock by half. Add the cream and mustards and leave in a warm place until needed.

For The Braised Baby Onions

Place the onions in a pan and cover with seasoned water. Bring to the boil, then turn the heat down and simmer until tender.

For The Turbot

Lightly flour and season the turbot and cook in a medium-hot frying pan. Colour for 2-3 minutes until golden. Turn the fish and remove the pan from the heat, allowing the excess heat from the pan to finish cooking the fish.

Chef's Tip

Try to use line caught turbot; it's a lot better for the environment.

For The Garnish

Whilst the turbot is cooking, roast the bacon and ceps with the braised baby onions in a medium-hot frying pan with a small amount of oil. When all nice and golden brown, add the wild garlic and wilt.

To Serve

Place the garnish in the middle of the plate, arrange the turbot on top and dress with the warm mustard sauce and chives.

GOAT'S CURD, SHROPSHIRE HONEY, LEMON, THYME

SERVES 4

Black Muscat, Quady Elysium, 2012
(California, USA)

Ingredients

120g goat's curd

Oat Crumble

40g oats
75g plain flour
60g Demerara sugar
60g unsalted butter
10g golden syrup
sea salt (pinch of)

Caramelised Oats

10g sugar, 25g honey
salt (pinch of)
5ml vegetable oil
75g jumbo oats

Honey Syrup

25g honey
10g liquid glucose
25g sugar, 25ml water
2 sprigs thyme (lemon thyme if possible)

Lemon Granita

50g sugar
200ml water
80ml lemon juice

Lemon Purée

4 lemons, 50g sugar
50ml water

Honey Gel

50g honey
25ml stock syrup
125ml water
10ml lemon juice
2g agar agar

Garnish

1 sprig thyme (lemon thyme if possible)

Method

For The Oat Crumble

Preheat the oven to 140°C (fan).
Mix all the dry ingredients together with the butter to breadcrumb stage. Add the syrup and mix again. Sprinkle the crumb mixture onto a lined baking tray and cook for 10-15 minutes until golden, stirring half way through. Set aside to cool. Store in an airtight container until needed.

For The Caramelised Oats

Preheat the oven to 140°C (fan).
Warm the sugar, honey, salt and oil in a pan to dissolve the sugar. Add the oats and stir well until evenly coated. Spread onto a lined baking tray and cook for 8-10 minutes until golden, stirring half way through. Set aside to cool. Store in an airtight container until needed.

For The Honey Syrup

Crush the sprigs of thyme and place in a pan with all the other ingredients. Warm to dissolve the sugar. Leave to infuse for 30 minutes, then pass through a sieve. Set aside until needed.

For The Lemon Granita

Put the sugar and water in a pan and warm to dissolve the sugar. Leave to cool slightly, then add the lemon juice. Place in the freezer. When the granita has started to freeze, scrape it with a fork. Repeat this until you are left with lemon crystals.

For The Lemon Purée

Warm the sugar and water in a pan to dissolve the sugar. Set aside.
Place the lemons in a pan and cover with cold water. Bring to the boil and simmer for 3 minutes. Repeat this process 10 times until the lemons are quite soft. Leave to cool, then remove the pips. Blend with the syrup until smooth. Pass through a sieve and set aside.

For The Honey Gel

Place everything in a pan and bring to the boil. Leave to cool - the agar agar will set the mixture. Once set, blend until smooth. Set aside until needed.

To Serve

Place a tablespoon of goat's curd in the middle of the plate. Cover with some of the oat crumble and caramelised oats. Dot the lemon purée and honey gel over the crumble. Pick a few leaves of thyme to scatter over. Drizzle with the syrup and place a tablespoon of the granita on top.

Chef's Tip

Source local honey and goat's curd; you will benefit from the flavour.

118
THE FOUR SEASONS RESTAURANT

Swinfen Hall Hotel, Swinfen, Near Lichfield, Staffordshire, WS14 9RE

01543 481 494
www.swinfenhallhotel.co.uk Twitter: @SwinfenHall @ProffittChef

When you step inside the grand lobby of this stunning 18th Century mansion it's easy to see why Swinfen Hall has been an AA Inspectors' Choice 4 Red Star hotel since 2007. Dig deeper and you will find the high ceilings and Georgian grandeur are merely scratching the surface of what Swinfen Hall has to offer.

Many restaurants liberally apply the terms local produce and seasonality to their menus, but in the case of The Four Seasons Restaurant at Swinfen Hall, the kitchens have a veritable larder in their 100 acre back garden.

The Victorian walled garden produces an abundance of organically grown vegetables and herbs as well as a wide range of soft and hard fruits, but that is far from all. The 45 acre deer park provides first class Sika venison and estate-reared lamb and hogget grace the menu, courtesy of a small flock of rare breed Manx Loaghtan sheep.

Head chef Paul Proffitt joined Swinfen in September 2013 at the tender age of 26 and within 15 months the restaurant was awarded 3 AA Rosettes and is currently the only restaurant in Staffordshire to hold this prestigious award. Paul is blessed with great imagination and drive as well as technical ability and his young and enthusiastic brigade produces innovative dishes, with a strong focus on delivering clean flavour combinations using a blend of contemporary and classic techniques.

Front of house, the restaurant team led by Pete Haw ensure guests receive a warm welcome and attentive personal service in the charming wood panelled dining room.

The combination of Georgian grandeur, Paul's creative approach to food and the bounty of produce grown and reared on the estate really makes The Four Seasons Restaurant at Swinfen Hall stand out from the crowd.

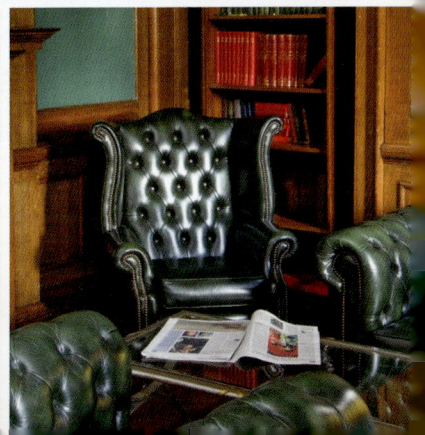

SWINFEN HALL HOTEL

HAND DIVED SCALLOP, CEVICHE, OCTOPUS CARPACCIO, WATERMELON, WASABI

SERVES 4

🍷 *Iron Stone Sauvignon Blanc 2007*
(California, USA)

Ingredients

Roast Scallop

4 large hand dived scallops
50ml vegetable oil
5g butter

Octopus Carpaccio

1 Mediterranean octopus (head removed)
1 lemon (zest and juice of)

Watermelon

1 small watermelon
100ml vegetable oil
1 lime (zest and juice of)

Wasabi Purée

200g rocket leaves (washed)
5g wasabi paste

Scallop Ceviche

2 large hand dived scallops (cut into small dice)
½ lime (juice and zest of)
25g fresh coriander (picked, chopped)
salt (to season)

Garnish

wasabi powder

Method

For The Octopus (Prepare ahead)

Place the octopus in a large saucepan with the lemon zest and juice. Cover with water and simmer for 60-75 minutes until tender. Remove the tentacles and place on a large sheet of cling film. Roll into a tight cylinder and refrigerate for 4-6 hours until set.

For The Watermelon

Slice the watermelon around 2cm thick. Cut out 20 different sized cylinders with round pastry cutters. Heavily burn 8 cylinders with a blow torch. Mix together the vegetable oil and lime with a hand blender and marinate 8 cylinders in this mix for 2 hours. Keep 4 more cylinders for garnish.

For The Wasabi Purée

Bring a large pan of water to the boil. Add in the rocket leaves and cook for 2-3 minutes. Place the leaves into a blender with the wasabi paste and blend until smooth. Pass through a sieve into a bowl and leave to cool, covered, in the fridge.

For The Scallop Ceviche

Combine the diced scallop, lime zest and juice and chopped coriander. Season with salt and set to one side for 10-15 minutes to marinate.

> **Chef's Tip**
> Hand dived scallops are superior in quality to their dredged counterparts and better for marine conservation, so try to use them if possible.

To Assemble

Cut 12 slices of the octopus and lay, overlapping, on the bottom of the plates. Place the various watermelon cylinders around the octopus. Add a few dots of the wasabi purée and small amounts of the scallop ceviche. Cut the 4 remaining scallops in half and roast in a very hot non-stick pan, presentation-side down. Add the butter and season the scallops before turning them over and draining on kitchen towel. Place 2 halves of the roast scallop in the centre of each plate. Garnish with wasabi powder.

RUMP & BREAST OF ESTATE REARED LAMB, BURNT GARLIC, AUBERGINE, ARTICHOKE, COAL OIL, BABY GEM

SERVES 4

Clos Du Val 2013, Zinfandel, Napa Valley, (California, USA)

Ingredients

Roast Lamb

4 lamb rumps (trimmed)

Lamb Breast

1 lamb breast (bones removed)
1 tsp salt

Coal Oil

5 large lumps of coal
250ml vegetable oil

Burnt Garlic Purée

6 bulbs garlic
300ml chicken stock

Aubergine

4 large aubergines
1 shallot (peeled, finely sliced)
1 clove garlic (peeled, finely sliced)
olive oil
salt (to season)

Artichoke

4 small globe artichokes
1 carrot (peeled, chopped)
1 small onion (peeled, chopped)
½ lemon (zest and juice of)
½ tsp coriander seeds (crushed)
1 star anise
100ml white wine
10ml white wine vinegar
200ml water

To Garnish

baby gem leaves
layers from a whole onion cooked in chicken stock

Method

For The Lamb Breast (Prepare the day before)

Preheat the oven to 140ºC.

Season the breast with salt and roll into a cylinder. Roll in cling film, then in foil. Place in the oven for 6 hours. Remove from the cling film and foil, then roll tightly into a cylinder using cling film and leave to set in the fridge overnight.

The Coal Oil (Prepare ahead)

Heat the coal until glowing white hot. Carefully drop the coal into the oil, in a heat proof container, and cover with foil to avoid setting the oil alight. Leave for 12 hours to infuse, then pass through a sieve.

For The Burnt Garlic Purée

Peel all the garlic and cut each clove in half. Burn half the garlic face down in a hot frying pan until completely black. Add this to the remaining garlic, cover with the chicken stock and simmer gently for 2-3 hours. Once tender, place in a blender and blend until smooth, then pass through a sieve.

For The Aubergine

Preheat the oven to 180ºC.

Bake the aubergines whole for 1 hour. Sauté the shallot and garlic in the olive oil until soft. Add the flesh from the baked aubergines and season with salt. Cook gently for 2-3 hours until the mix is deep brown in colour and slightly sticky.

For The Artichoke

Peel the outer leaves off the artichokes and remove the fluffy core. Trim and place in a pan with all the ingredients. Simmer gently until the artichokes are tender. Allow to cool in the liquor.

To Serve

Roast the lamb rumps gently in a frying pan, fat-side down to crisp up the fat. Turn over and cook until pink, then leave to rest. Cut rounds of the lamb breast and fry until crispy. Assemble as pictured.

> **Chef's Tip**
>
> If you are struggling to find lamb rumps, this dish will also work well with a more readily available rack or loin of lamb.

LEMON CURD, LEMON MACARON, PARMA VIOLET, LEMON BALM

SERVES 4

Araldica Moscato Passito 2010, Palazzina
(Italy)

Ingredients

Lemon Curd

270ml lemon juice
7g agar agar
270g whole eggs (about 5 eggs)
270g caster sugar
350g salted butter

Macarons

125g egg whites
40g caster sugar
3g yellow food colouring powder
225g icing sugar
125g ground almonds

Parma Violet Ice Cream

220g Parma Violet sweets (crushed)
280ml semi-skimmed milk
280ml double cream
8 egg yolks (beaten)
2 drops violet food colouring

To Garnish

violet flowers
lemon balm
Parma Violet sweets (crushed)

30 x 15 x 4cm mould (lined with cling film)

Method

For The Lemon Curd

Bring the lemon juice and agar agar to the boil. Remove from the heat and allow to cool slightly. Mix in the eggs and sugar and whisk over a pan of simmering water until thick. Remove from the heat and whisk in the butter until thoroughly combined and dissolved. Pour into the prepared mould and leave in the fridge to set.

Chef's Tip

If you can't find agar agar in your local supermarket, it can normally be found in health food shops.

For The Macarons

Whisk the egg whites to stiff peaks, then add in the caster sugar and food colouring. Blend the almonds and icing sugar and pass through a sieve. Mix the egg whites with the sugar and almonds and stir until the mix just falls off the spoon. Put in a piping bag and pipe into 2cm rounds on a non-stick mat. Leave for 3 hours at room temperature.

Preheat the oven to 120°C.

Transfer the macarons to the oven and cook for 30-35 minutes.

For The Parma Violet Ice Cream

Gently heat the crushed sweets with the milk and cream until the sweets have dissolved. Pour the mix over the beaten egg yolks and mix well. Return to the pan and cook very gently, so as not to scramble the eggs, until the mix becomes thick enough to coat the back of a spoon. Add in the colouring and leave in the fridge to cool. Churn in an ice cream machine.

To Serve

Whip half of the lemon curd in a mixer until very pale and light. Sandwich a small amount of this mixture between the macaron shells. Cut the remaining curd into sharp rectangles and place in the centre of the plate. Dust the plate with the crushed sweets, violet flowers and lemon balm. Place the macaron standing up and finish the dish with a scoop of ice cream as pictured.

128
THE GREAT HALL
AT THE LYGON ARMS

Broadway, Worcestershire, WR12 7DU

01386 852 255
www.thehotelcollection.co.uk/hotels/the-lygon-arms-hotel-cotswolds Twitter: @The_LygonArms

n the heart of Broadway is The Lygon Arms, a traditional coaching inn, rich in history and charm. The Inn is also an internationally renowned 4 star hotel, led by general manager Colin Heaney, with an enviable reputation for the finest cuisine and the best of 21st Century comforts. It has four acres of grounds which include lawns, flower gardens, croquet and floodlit tennis for the exclusive use of guests. The Lygon Arms also has its own spa and conference facilities. The Great Hall restaurant offers guests a 2 AA Rosette dining experience, or for those looking for less formality, there is Barrington's Brasserie and, when the sun shines, the outside courtyard too.

Relaxing in front of large open fires, you can easily feel like you have drifted back in time to a bygone era. The Inn is steeped in history and first appeared in the parish register in 1532.

In the 17th Century, it served both sides of the Civil War; Oliver Cromwell stayed here before the decisive battle of Worcester in 1651 and Charles I also used The Inn to meet his supporters. In more recent times, celebrities such as Elizabeth Taylor and Richard Burton have visited.

Nestled in the Cotswolds, 'an area of outstanding natural beauty', on the doorstep of The Vale of Evesham, 'the fruit and vegetable basket of England', with local produce and stunning views in abundance. The Inn is the perfect place to escape the maddening crowd!

Ales Maurer and his chefs have kept a consistent high standard of 2 AA Rosettes by using old and new cooking techniques, appreciating fresh flavours and seasonal produce.

THE
LYGON
ARMS

HERITAGE TOMATO JELLY & PRESSING, BALSAMIC ICE CREAM, GOAT'S CURD

SERVES 4

Mâcon Villages (France)

Ingredients

Tomato Jelly
10 vine tomatoes (diced)
½ stick celery (peeled)
2 cloves garlic (chopped)
3 spring onions (chopped)
4 red peppers (chopped)
1 litre tomato juice
chilli powder (pinch of), salt and pepper
3 tbsp Worcester sauce
8 gelatine leaves (softened)

Tomato Pressing
20 vine tomatoes (quartered, seeds removed)
2 leeks, salt, pepper and sugar (to season)
tomato jelly (see above)

Ginger Pesto
1 root ginger (peeled), 1 clove garlic
rocket (handful of), 100ml olive oil

Red Pepper Coulis
3 red peppers, 1 clove garlic
sugar (to taste), 2 tsp water

Ceviche
mini heritage tomatoes (selection of)
ginger pesto, red pepper coulis, olive oil

Balsamic Butter Ice Cream
165g caster sugar
600ml full-fat milk (hot)
75g butter, 6 egg yolks
1 tbsp cornflour
4 tbsp balsamic vinegar

To Serve
goat's curd
brioche crumbs, sea salt
watercress

muslin, terrine mould (lined with cling film)

Method

For The Tomato Jelly (Prepare 2 days before)
Blitz the vegetables to a purée, then add all the other ingredients, except the gelatine. Pour into lined muslin and leave to drip overnight into a container. Warm the liquid, add the gelatine leaves, then strain through a fine *chinois*. Cut 12 cubes from the set jelly and set aside.

> **Chef's Tip**
> When heating the water for the tomato jelly, do not boil or it goes cloudy. For more colour in the tomato pressing, add basil leaves.

For The Tomato Pressing (Prepare ahead)
Preheat the oven to 170°C (fan).
Dry roast the seasoned tomatoes, flesh side up, for 15 minutes. Wash and separate the leaves from the leeks. *Blanch* in boiling water until softened and still green, then refresh and dry on a cloth. Place the leek leaves in the mould leaving an overhang. Melt the remaining tomato jelly in a pan and pour a small amount to cover the base. Layer tomatoes skin-side up, pressing as you go and adding a small ladle of jelly liquid between each layer. Fold the leeks over the final layer of tomatoes. Pull cling film over to tighten and press with another terrine mould for 12 hours.

For The Ginger Pesto
Blitz the ginger, garlic and rocket in a food processor. Gradually add the olive oil while mixing.

For The Red Pepper Coulis
Preheat the oven to 170°C (fan).
Roast the peppers for 15 minutes. Leave to cool, then remove the skins and seeds. Blitz in a processor with the garlic and sugar, adding water to achieve a smooth consistency.

For The Ceviche
Halve and quarter the tomatoes to give a variety of sizes. Dress with a little ginger pesto, red pepper coulis and olive oil.

For The Balsamic Butter Ice Cream
Caramelise 150g of the sugar and pour onto the hot milk. Make a *beurre noisette* with the butter and pass through a sieve. Whisk the yolks and the remaining sugar until fluffy, then add the cornflour. Add to the caramelised milk mixture, then whisk in the butter and balsamic vinegar. Churn, then freeze.

To Assemble The Dish
Remove the pressing from the mould and slice. Place on a plate and sprinkle with sea salt. Decorate with ceviche, jelly cubes, a scoop of balsamic ice cream, *quenelles* of goat's curd and garnish as pictured. Serve immediately.

QUAIL & PORK, BEETROOT, CAVOLO NERO, APPLE JUS

SERVES 4

Callia Malbec, 2014
(Argentina)

Ingredients

Pork Belly

500g pork belly (with fat)
3 litres apple juice
10g sea salt
2 cloves
4 sage leaves

Quail

4 whole quail
1 orange (zest and juice of)
1 egg
1 clove garlic
25g fresh tarragon
8 slices pancetta

Apple Jus

quail and pork bones
1 clove garlic
200ml apple juice

Beetroot

1kg heritage beetroot (red, candy stripe and golden)
100ml orange juice
30g sugar

Potatoes

2 large potatoes (peeled, sliced thinly)

Garnish

1 large cavolo nero
butter (knob of)
4 quail eggs
salt (pinch of)
seeds and nuts

Method

For The Pork Belly (Prepare ahead)

Preheat the oven to 180°C (fan).

Roast the pork belly for 20 minutes. Sprinkle with sea salt, cover with apple juice, then add the cloves and sage. Reduce the oven to 110°C (fan) and cook for a further 7 hours.

For The Quail

Debone the quail and separate the breasts from the legs. Blend the leg meat, orange zest and juice, egg, garlic and tarragon in a food processor. Pipe the mousse into the middle of the 2 breasts and roll together using 2 slices of pancetta. Repeat for the other breasts. Wrap separately in cling film, poach gently for 10 minutes, then colour in a hot pan.

> **Chef's Tip**
>
> Add pork belly trimmings to your quail mousse to enhance the flavour and moisture.

For The Apple Jus

Preheat the oven to 180°C (fan).

Roast the quail and pork bones until golden brown, about 10 minutes. Add with the garlic and apple juice to a pan and reduce. Pass through a fine sieve and keep warm.

For The Beetroot

Use your imagination with the colours of beetroot. Boil with the orange juice and sugar, then peel and slice 2 of the beets to use in the potatoes. With the remaining beets, dice, slice, grate, pickle and go wild!

For The Potatoes (Prepare ahead)

Preheat the oven to 180°C (fan).

Cook the potato slices between 2 trays for 15 minutes, then roll with the sliced beetroot. When cool, cut into portions. Reheat to serve.

For The Garnish

Soften the cavolo nero in butter, fry the quail eggs, blitz the seeds and nuts and arrange on the plate as pictured.

EVESHAM STRAWBERRIES, ELDERFLOWER & MASCARPONE, MINT

SERVES 8

🍷 *Concha Y Toro Late Harvest, Sauvignon Blanc
(Chile)*

Ingredients

Elderflower And Mascarpone Mousse

150g mascarpone
100g cream cheese
55g crème fraîche
35g sugar
1 vanilla pod (seeds of)
30ml elderflower cordial
2 leaves bronze gelatine (soaked in cold water)

Strawberry Gel

125g strawberry purée
1¾g agar agar

Sorbet Syrup

315g sugar
190ml water

Strawberry Sorbet

250g strawberry purée
160ml sorbet syrup
80ml water

Garnish

strawberries
mint leaves
strawberry crisps
edible flowers
sugar shards

Method

For The Strawberry Gel

Add the agar agar to the cold strawberry purée and mix until dissolved. Heat slowly and gently boil for 5 minutes, whisking so it doesn't catch. Pour half the liquid into a small, shallow tray lined with cling film. Leave to set.

For The Elderflower And Mascarpone Mousse

Blend the mascarpone, cream cheese, crème fraîche, sugar and seeds from the vanilla pod in a food processor. Heat the elderflower cordial and dissolve the gelatine in it. Add the elderflower to the food processor and blend again.

Pour onto the strawberry gel. Place in the fridge and leave to set for 3-4 hours. Reheat the remaining strawberry gel very gently and pour on top of the mascarpone.

For The Sorbet Syrup

Mix the sugar and water and slowly bring to the boil. Boil for 5 minutes.

For The Strawberry Sorbet

Mix the ingredients together, churn in an ice cream machine and freeze.

To Garnish And Assemble

Cut the mascarpone into squares and arrange on desired plates. Use fresh local strawberries to garnish and strawberry crisps. Finish with mint and strawberry sorbet.

> **Chef's Tip**
> Have patience with this recipe, the end result will be worth it!

138
THE OLD BAKERY
RESTAURANT WITH ROOMS

26/28 Burton Road, Lincoln, LN1 3LB

01522 576 057
www.theold-bakery.co.uk Twitter: @theoldbakeryuk

The Old Bakery Restaurant with Rooms, owned by Tracey and Ivano de Serio, situated directly in the centre of Lincoln's historic district is proud not only to serve quality food but the team also create a memorable and personal dining experience.

The Old Bakery's reputation rests on both its dedication to serving the finest standard of à la carte dining and the ever-changing and exciting tasting menus, personally crafted by Ivano de Serio and individually paired with accompanying wines for each course. Prepared under modern and cutting-edge techniques, the food nevertheless retains all the comfort and pleasure of the most traditional of Italian recipes.

Trained in Puglia, Italy, head chef patron Ivano's experience in freshly made, locally sourced cuisine is a passion shared by all staff in this family-run restaurant, operating to the highest standards of quality and specialist dining since 2004.

An historic building, flavoured with the redolent nature of original flooring and perfectly preserved baking ovens, The Old Bakery merges a modern, airy conservatory in the walled garden seamlessly with the rustic, comfortable atmosphere of the front dining area.

As with the restaurant and cuisine, the accommodation is the perfect blend of both modern and traditional themes, respecting and complementing the historic nature of the building, whilst employing light and space for a peaceful and relaxing visit.

The Old Bakery is proud to play host to evenings dedicated to the joys of food, drink, and music. Its Balvenie evening, which saw the famous whisky paired with a specially designed tasting menu, was merely one example of the dedication to exploring new ways to satisfy the palate and the brain.

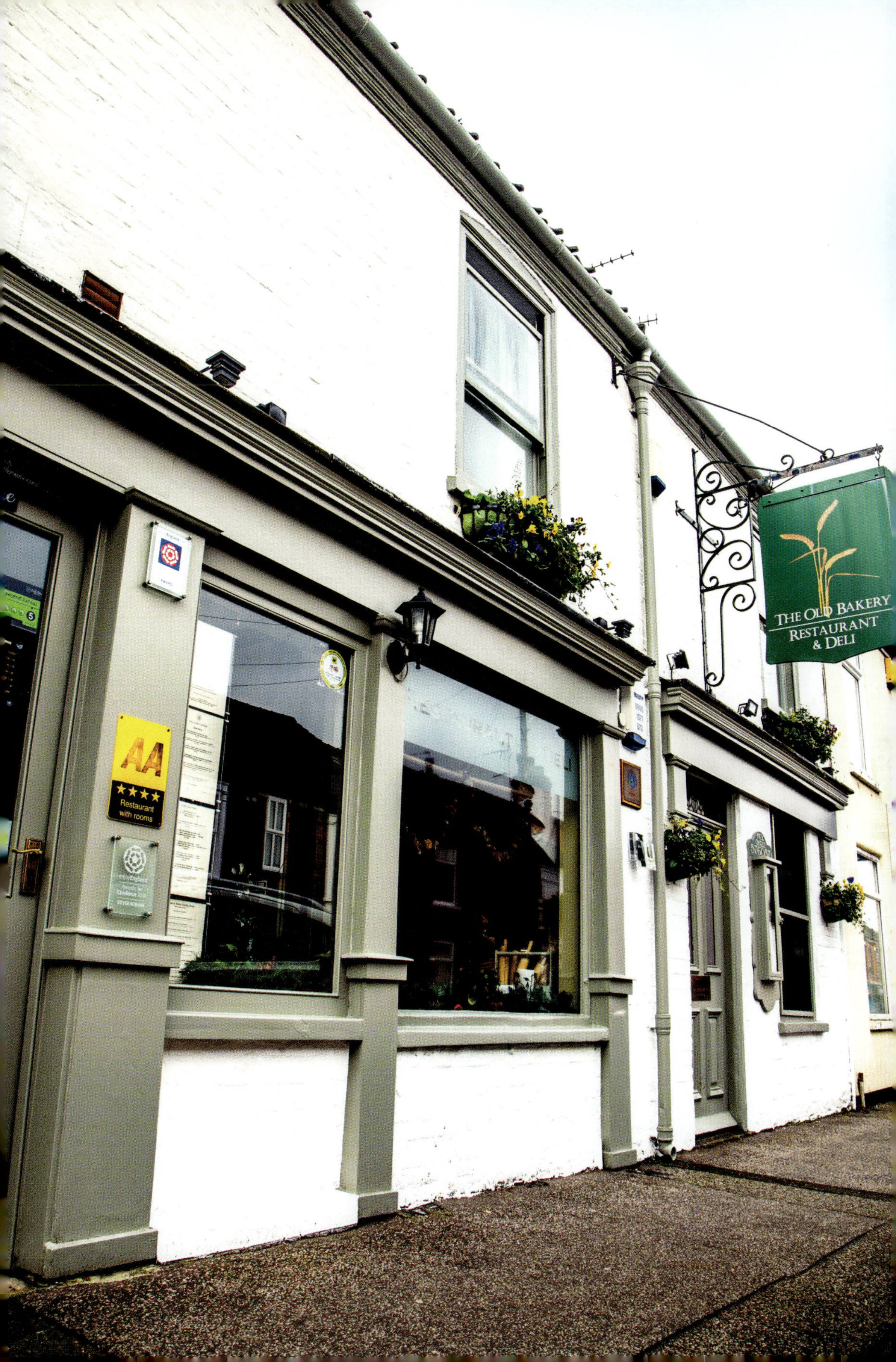
THE OLD BAKERY
RESTAURANT
& DELI
AA
★★★★
Restaurant
with rooms

As the only restaurant in Lincoln to hold 2 AA Rosette Awards, The Old Bakery's passion for excellent food is displayed in regular cookery lessons, taught by Ivano, who takes pride in instructing and educating in the nature of professional cuisine.

CUTTLEFISH & PANCETTA ARANCINI, CRAB BISQUE, GRANNY SMITH APPLE

SERVES 4

New Hall Bacchus
(Essex, England)

Ingredients

Crab Bisque

2 x 500g live stone crabs
250ml dry white wine
8 bay leaves
10 whole black peppercorns
100g butter
1 head celery (chopped)
2 onions (diced), 2 carrots (diced)
2 Granny Smith apples (cut into wedges, skin on)
100ml brandy, water (to cover)
100g tomato purée
100g rice flour
200ml double cream
salt and ground white pepper (to taste)
2 lemons (juice of)

Cuttlefish And Pancetta Arancini

50g unsalted butter
2 small onions (finely chopped)
200g smoked pancetta (diced)
2 cloves garlic (chopped)
250g rice (arborio, carnaroli or vialone nano)
30g cuttlefish ink
200ml white wine
2 litres vegetable stock (warm)
salt and freshly ground black pepper
150g Parmesan cheese (grated)
2 eggs (beaten)
100ml cold water
200g plain flour, 300g breadcrumbs
1 litre vegetable oil (for deep frying)

Granny Smith Apple

2 Granny Smith apples
1 lemon (juice of)
2 lovage leaves (chopped)
50ml extra virgin avocado oil

Garnish

100g fresh peas (cooked)

Method

For The Crab Bisque

Fill a deep pan three quarters full with water. Add the white wine, bay leaves and peppercorns and bring to the boil. Add the live crabs and cook for about 20 minutes. Remove the crabs and allow to cool down before extracting the meat.

Meanwhile, in a heavy bottomed, deep pan, add the butter, celery, onions and carrots and cook for 5 minutes. Add the crab shells and the apple wedges. Stir in the brandy and *flambé*. Add the water and tomato purée and simmer for 1½ hours. Strain the liquid, mix the rice flour with the cream and add to the cooking liquid. Season with salt, pepper and lemon juice.

For The Cuttlefish And Pancetta Arancini

Melt the butter in a large, heavy bottomed saucepan. Add the onions, pancetta and garlic and cook for 2-3 minutes on a medium heat. Stir in the rice. When it starts to become a little translucent around the edges, add the ink and wine. Add a ladleful of warm stock and stir well. When the stock has almost been absorbed, add another ladleful. Continue adding more stock until it has all been added and the rice is cooked. Season with salt and freshly ground black pepper. Add the Parmesan and set aside to cool.

Combine the eggs with a little salt and 100ml cold water. Sprinkle the flour onto a plate.

Roll the rice into small balls, dredge in the flour, dip into the beaten egg and then the breadcrumbs.

Half fill a deep, heavy bottomed saucepan with vegetable oil and heat to 170°C.

Deep fry the arancini for 3-4 minutes, or until golden brown. Remove from the oil using a slotted spoon and set aside to drain on kitchen paper.

For The Granny Smith Apple

Julienne the apples using a mandolin. Place in a bowl with the lemon juice, avocado oil and lovage. Mix gently.

> **Chef's Tip**
>
> Prepare the apple *julienne* 15 minutes before serving so the lovage will stay green and fresh.

To Serve

Place the apple *julienne* in the centre of the plate. Pour the bisque, add the peas, crabmeat and arancini as pictured.

LINCOLNSHIRE FALLOW DEER LOIN, SMOKED POTATO, SQUASH PORRIDGE, BITTER CHOCOLATE OIL

SERVES 4

*Malvasia Nera, Cantine San Marzano
(Puglia, Italy)*

Ingredients

Venison

1 x 800g venison sirloin
ground juniper berries (pinch of)
salt (pinch of)

Chocolate Oil

50g 75-80% cocoa solids dark chocolate (chopped)
100ml corn oil
Maldon smoked salt (pinch of)

Smoked Potato

4 large King Edward potatoes (peeled, shaped)
100ml rice vinegar
30g oak smoking dust
50ml rapeseed oil
salt (to taste)

Squash Porridge

50g butternut squash (small dice)
75g butter
1 small shallot (chopped)
½ clove garlic (chopped)
ground nutmeg (pinch of)
50ml dry vermouth
100g porridge oats
300ml strong venison or beef stock
50ml double cream
salt (to taste)

To Serve

Swiss chard (wilted)

Method

For The Venison (Prepare the day before)

Trim the loin, salt and season all over with the ground juniper berries. Roll very tightly in cling film and refrigerate overnight.

3 hours before service, heat a water bath to 60½°C. Place the wrapped loin in a zip bag and immerse in the water bath for 2½ hours.

Alternatively, sear the venison as above, then place in a preheated oven, 190°C (fan), for 3-4 minutes, or longer if you like the meat medium.

Set aside to rest for 1 minute before slicing.

For The Chocolate Oil

Gently heat the oil with the salt, add the chocolate and slowly melt on a very low heat. Take off the stove and keep at room temperature in a plastic container with a lid until needed.

For The Smoked Potato

Bring a large, shallow pan with water, rice vinegar, rapeseed oil, and salt to the boil.

Shape the potatoes as pictured and cook on a medium heat for 5-6 minutes.

Gently drain the potatoes and place them in a stove smoker with the smoking dust. Lightly wet with water. Cover and cook on a medium heat for 4 minutes.

Remove from the heat and leave the potato to infuse with the smoke until needed.

For The Squash Porridge

Melt the butter in a heavy bottomed pan, add the shallot and squash and cook on low for 2-3 minutes. Add the garlic and nutmeg, stir in the vermouth and cook for 1 minute. Add the oats and the stock. Cook on low for 2 minutes. Pour in the cream and season with salt, if necessary.

Chef's Tip

The longer the oil infuses, the better the flavour. Make sure you prepare the porridge immediately prior to serving.

To Serve

When ready to serve, heat a non-stick pan on a medium heat, add the chocolate oil and pan roast the venison for 20 seconds on each side. Plate as pictured.

CHOCOLATE WHISKY CAKE, WHITE CHOCOLATE MASCARPONE MOUSSE, CHOCOLATE SOIL & WHISKY JELLY

SERVES 6

Balvenie 14 Year Old Rum Cask Whisky (Scotland)

Ingredients

White Chocolate Mascarpone Mousse

250g mascarpone cheese (room temperature)
80ml warm milk
1 gelatine leaf (soaked in cold water)
90g white chocolate
50g icing sugar

Whisky Jelly

75ml Balvenie DoubleWood 17 year old malt whisky
75ml clear apple juice
15ml verjus
2 star anise, 2 cloves
1 gelatine leaf (soaked in cold water)

Chocolate Whisky Cake

10g cocoa powder (Extra Brute)
220g granulated sugar
85g plain flour, 450ml milk
70g butter
100g dark chocolate (64%)
100g eggs
40g egg yolks
20ml Balvenie Caribbean Cask 14 year old whisky

Chocolate Soil

200g granulated sugar
200g ground almonds
120g plain flour
90g cocoa powder (Extra Brute)
140g butter (melted, cooled)
12g salt

To Garnish

passion fruit meringue (optional)
edible flowers

6 miniature plum cake moulds (greased with oil spray)

Method

For The White Chocolate Mascarpone Mousse
(Prepare in advance)

Bring the milk to a simmer, remove from the heat and stir in the gelatine.

Melt the white chocolate in a *bain-marie*, then add the warm milk.

Whisk the mascarpone with the icing sugar. Pour in the chocolate mixture while the mixer is on a high speed. Pass through a sieve into a container with lid. Refrigerate for 4-5 hours, or overnight.

For The Whisky Jelly

Place all the ingredients, except for the gelatine, in a pan and gently heat to 85°C. Remove from the heat and add the gelatine. Leave for 20 minutes. Strain into a cling film lined container and refrigerate for 2-3 hours.

For The Chocolate Whisky Cake

Preheat the oven to 180°C (fan).

Sift the cocoa powder, sugar and flour together.

Bring the milk to the boil and pour it on top of the butter and chocolate in a bowl. Stir until the butter and chocolate are melted and combined.

Beat the eggs and yolks, then whisk into the sifted flour mix to form a paste.

Combine the chocolate and egg mixtures together, then add the whisky.

Fill the moulds to ½cm from the top. Bake for 45-50 minutes. The cake should feel firm when pressed with a fingertip.

> **Chef's Tip**
>
> The chocolate cake mixture will be very runny, but that is normal - do not worry. Remove the cakes from the moulds before they cool completely.

For The Chocolate Soil

Preheat the oven at 160°C (fan). Mix all the ingredients in a mixer bowl with a paddle attachment until fully combined. Spread in an even layer on a baking tray lined with non-stick baking parchment. Bake for 15 minutes, or until aromatic. Cool and reserve in an airtight container in the fridge.

To Serve

Serve as pictured.

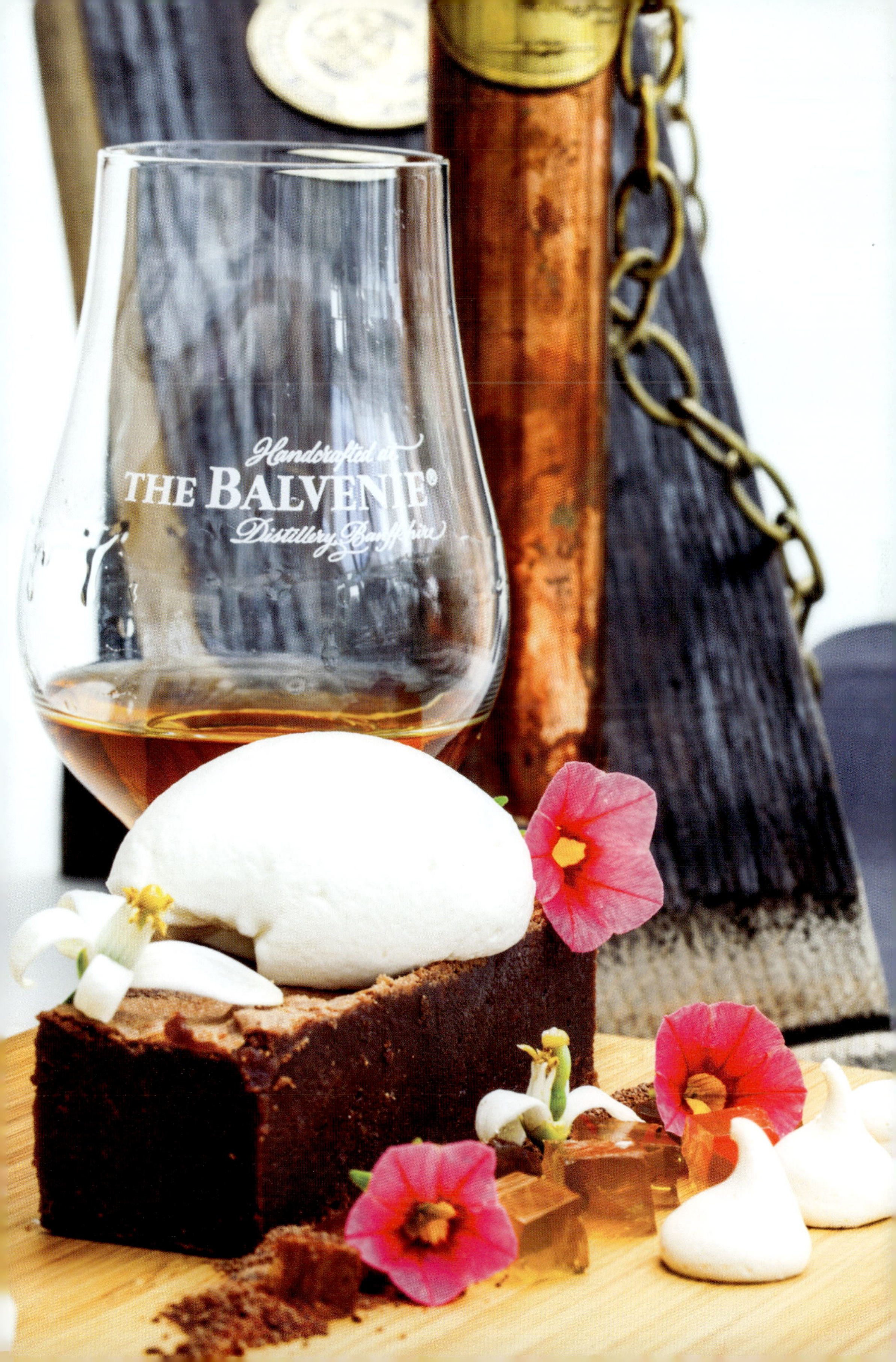
Handcrafted at
THE BALVENIE®
Distillery Banffshire

148
OLD DOWNTON LODGE

Downton-On-The-Rock, Ludlow, SY8 2HU

01568 771 826
www.olddowntonlodge.com Twitter: @olddowntonlodge

Old Downton Lodge, restaurant with rooms, is a 3 AA Rosette award-winning establishment and a new listed entry in the Michelin Guide for 2016, situated just six miles from Ludlow. Boasting a total of nine luxury bedrooms, the lodge is set amongst a mixture of converted farm buildings; medieval, half timbered and Georgian - all of which surround a herb and flower bedecked courtyard peering over the Hereford hills. This is an establishment of pure escapism; a chance to immerse oneself in rich history and a memorable fine-dining experience.

In the sitting room, mighty timbers that once fronted dairy stalls now provide seating from which to watch the roaring log burner, socialise, and enjoy a drink from the bar. The museum, with its huge cider apple mill, provides a dramatic focal point to a room ideal for small, intimate weddings, conferences and private parties.

The dining room radiates the aura of a grand medieval hall. In fact, it was built around the time of the Norman Conquest. However, the small triangular windows suggest a more prosaic history.

What you probably won't see is the kitchen, where head chef Karl Martin is paring down the choice of stunning fresh local produce - there's so much to choose from.

Karl produces a daily changing tasting menu, drawing his inspiration from local market produce, the kitchen garden and foraging expeditions across the Herefordshire countryside. Dinner is served from Tuesday to Saturday, between 6pm and 9pm.

Owners Pippa and Willem Vlok are very hands on with Old Downton Lodge, both running the front of house whilst Karl runs the kitchen. This combination saw them win 3 AA Rosettes and a listing in the Michelin Guide 2016.

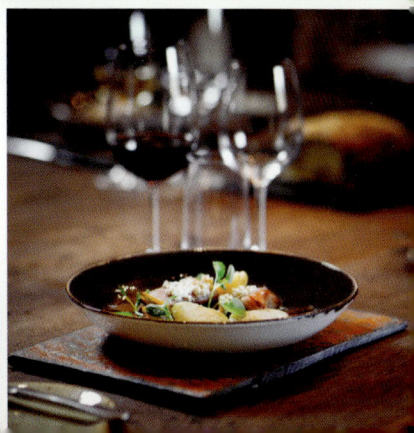

ASPARAGUS & GRAPES WITH TRUFFLE & PARMESAN CUSTARD

SERVES 4

Mâcon-Lugny, Les Genièvres, Louis Latour 2012, (France)

Ingredients

20 grapes

Truffle And Parmesan Custard

50ml milk
2g agar agar
1 egg
50g butter
50g grated Parmesan
10ml truffle oil
salt (to taste)

Asparagus

12 spears asparagus
salt and pepper
olive oil (to drizzle)

Grape Gel

100g grapes
2g agar agar

Roasted Walnuts

50g walnuts
20g butter
salt (to taste)

Garnish

wild chervil

Method

For The Grapes (Prepare ahead)

Preheat the oven to 100°C (fan).

Remove the grapes from their stalks and place in the oven for around 4-5 hours.

> **Chef's Tip**
> Allow at least 5 hours to bake the grapes.

For The Truffle And Parmesan Custard

Place the milk and agar agar in a saucepan on a low heat and whisk until dissolved.

Boil for 2 minutes, add the egg and scramble. Bring back to the boil, then remove from the heat and add the remaining ingredients, seasoning with salt to taste.

Blend the mixture, then leave to set in the fridge for 3 hours.

Once set, place back into the blender and blitz to a smooth paste.

To Cook The Asparagus

Snap the asparagus and discard the woody part, leaving the tender spears.

Trim 20 (5 per person) ½cm slices from the bottom of the spears. Set aside until ready to serve.

Chargrill the asparagus spears, turning every minute or so until coloured round the edge. Season with salt and pepper and drizzle with olive oil.

For The Grape Gel

Blend the grapes until smooth, then add the grape mix and agar agar to a pan and bring to the boil. Allow to boil for 2 minutes, then remove from the heat. Place in the fridge for 2 hours. Once it has set hard, blend again to a smooth paste. Pass the paste through a sieve and place in a piping bag until ready to serve.

For The Roasted Walnuts

Preheat the oven to 175°C (fan).

Blend the walnuts using the pulse setting on a blender until a tenth of the size. Scatter the blended walnuts on a tray with the butter and salt and bake in the oven for a few minutes until golden brown. Drain and leave to cool before serving.

To Serve

Arrange the cooked asparagus on the plate, then add the custard, walnuts, the grape gel and dehydrated grapes around the asparagus. Finish with the raw asparagus and wild chervil.

SHROPSHIRE LAMB RUMP & SHOULDER, GARLIC & PEA PUREE, BABY GEM LETTUCE

SERVES 4

Viña Salceda Reserva, Rioja 2009
(Spain)

Ingredients

Lamb

500g lamb rump
500g lamb shoulder
3 sprigs thyme
lamb bones (from shoulder)
1 bulb garlic
salt (to season)

Garlic Purée

2 cloves garlic (peeled)
milk (splash of)

Pea Purée

200g frozen peas (defrosted)
water (splash of)
salt (to season)

Baby Gem Lettuce

1-2 baby gem lettuce
rapeseed oil
salt (to season)

Garnish

100g raw peas (shelled)
rock samphire

Method

To Cook The Lamb Shoulder (Prepare ahead)

Preheat the oven to 140°C (fan).

Seal the lamb shoulder in a pan until it turns a golden brown colour. Transfer to a deep baking tray. Add the thyme, lamb bones, garlic and water to cover.

Cook for around 5 hours until very tender.

Remove from the tray. Pull the lamb apart a little, then add some of the cooking stock for moisture. Season, then roll with cling film into a cylinder shape. Leave to cool in the fridge until ready to serve.

> **Chef's Tip**
> Allow plenty of time to cook the lamb shoulder.

To Cook The Lamb Rump

Remove the bark (thin layer of skin on top of the lamb) and place in a vacuum pack bag. Cook in a water bath at 56°C for 90 minutes. Alternatively, preheat the oven to 180°C (fan) and cook for 15-20 minutes depending on size.

Once cooked, season and seal the fat side of the rump in a hot pan. When golden brown, place to the side and allow to rest for 5-10 minutes before plating.

For The Garlic Purée

Blanch the peeled garlic 3 times. When tender, remove from the water and blitz. Add a splash of milk until a smooth purée forms. Season, then pass through a sieve.

For The Pea Purée

Place the defrosted peas in a blender with a splash of water and blitz until smooth. Season to taste.

For The Baby Gem Lettuce

Cut each lettuce into 4 and cook in a hot pan with the rapeseed oil and season. When brown on one side, turn and colour the other side.

To Serve

Plate as pictured. Drizzle with the braising juices.

CHERRIES, BASIL, PISTACHIO

SERVES 4

*Vondeling Sweet Carolyn 2009
(Western Cape)*

Ingredients

Cherry Sorbet

65g cherry purée
25g caster sugar
25g trimoline invert sugar
65ml water

Cherry Marshmallow

3 sheets gelatine (soaked in cold water)
100g egg whites (pasteurised)
200g caster sugar
50ml water
cherry purée (to taste)

Cherry Gel

100g cherry purée
2g agar agar

Pickled Cherries

100ml water
50g sugar
100ml white wine vinegar
12 cherries (halved, de-stoned)

Roasted Pistachios

150g pistachios (shelled)
oil (to drizzle)
salt (pinch of)

Garnish

basil cress

Method

For The Cherry Sorbet (Prepare in advance)

Place all the ingredients in a pan and bring to a simmer. Set aside to cool. Once cooled, add the mix to an ice cream machine and churn to the manufacturer's instructions. Leave in the freezer until ready to serve.

Chef's Tip

Make the sorbet the night before.

To Make The Cherry Marshmallow

Whisk the egg whites and 35g of the caster sugar into soft peaks. Combine the remaining sugar and water in a pan and bring to 116ºC. Stir in the softened gelatine, then slowly add to the egg whites, whisking continuously.

Keep whisking until it cools, then slowly add the cherry purée.

Once completely cool, set in a tray lined with cling film. Place in the fridge for 2 hours until ready to serve.

For The Cherry Gel

Whisk the cherry purée and agar agar in a pan and boil for 2 minutes. Remove from the heat and place in a container in the fridge for 2 hours.

Once set, remove from the container and blitz to a smooth paste. Keep cool in the fridge until ready to plate.

For The Pickled Cherries

Mix the water, sugar and vinegar in a pan and bring to the boil. Remove from the heat, then add the halved cherries. Leave to cool.

For The Roasted Pistachios

Preheat the oven to 170ºC (fan).

Roast the pistachios with a drizzle of oil and a pinch of salt until they start to turn brown, about 5-7 minutes.

Remove from the oven and drain on a towel. Leave to cool before serving.

To Serve

Plate as pictured and garnish with basil cress.

158
THE PEACH TREE

18 Abbey Foregate, Shrewsbury, SY2 6AE

01743 355 055
www.thepeachtree.co.uk Twitter: @ThePeachTree1

Shrewsbury has one of the Midlands' most vibrant and eclectic gastronomic cultures.

The picturesque Shropshire market town has a thriving food scene with dozens of independent restaurants. Foremost among them is The Peach Tree, on Wyle Cop, near to Shrewsbury's Abbey. The Peach Tree is part of a group of three independent restaurants. Its sister restaurants are Momo No Ki, a Japanese ramen noodle bar, and Havana Republic, which celebrates the flavours of Cuba.

Executive head chef Chris Burt oversees all three restaurants, bringing a lifetime of travel to the pass.

Burt spent much of his youth in Africa and has since been on the road, travelling through many parts of Asia and America. In recent times, he has completed stages at some of the best restaurants in the world, particularly in New York, and he brings his experience to bear with instinctive off the cuff combinations at The Peach Tree, Momo No Ki and Havana Republic.

He said: "We have a unique operation here in Shrewsbury. We're serving quick, tasty, affordable flavours from around the world.

"But our provenance is second to none. We've got all sorts of suppliers who are growing, rearing and breeding especially for us. We're changing the menu not by the seasons, but by the day. We're working with the region's best artisans. We've got a passionate, creative and hard working team."

Momo No Ki was created following one of Burt's many road trips through Japan. "I spent a lot of research and development time in Japan and was totally inspired." His customers have been, too.

Award-winning executive head chef Chris Burt oversees The Peach Tree, Momo No Ki and Havana Republic. "We have a unique operation here in Shrewsbury. We're serving quick, tasty, affordable flavours from around the world."

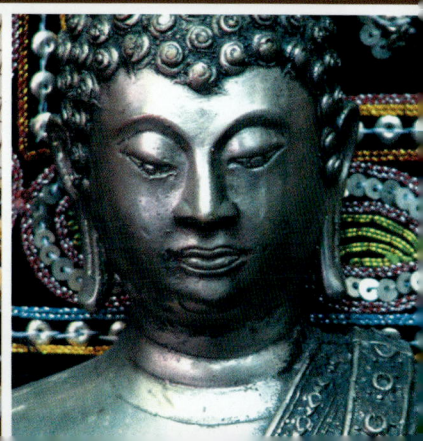

THE EARTH & THE SEA

Momo No Ki
19 Abbey Foregate, Shrewsbury, SY2 6AE
01743 281 770 www.momonoki.co.uk Twitter: @MomoNoKiRamen

SERVES 2

Erdener Treppchen Riesling Kabinett, Meulenhof, Mosel 2014 (Germany)

Ingredients

Dashi

500ml dashi
kombu (1 piece)
3 shiitake mushrooms
800g plum or beef tomatoes (chopped)
1 tbsp katsuobushi

Shiitake Mushrooms

shiitake mushrooms (handful of)
rice wine vinegar (to cover)
soy sauce (to taste)
mirin (a few splashes of)

Scallops

2 scallops
rapeseed oil

To Serve

samphire
seasonal sea herbs
1 tsp caviar

Garnish

nasturtium flowers
chilli shrimp oil
red-vein sorrel

Method

For The Dashi (Prepare ahead)

Simmer the dashi, then add the kombu and infuse. Add the shiitake mushrooms and 200g of the tomatoes. Simmer lightly, then remove from the heat and strain. Add the katsuobushi to your warm dashi and leave for between 3-5 minutes, depending on how smoky you like it. Drain, then simmer the dashi very, very slowly, until reduced by half. Leave to stand.

Blend the remaining tomatoes in a food processor. Strain through muslin for at least 12 hours. Add the resulting pure tomato essence to your dashi and simmer to reduce by half. You will be left with a very light, vibrant and clear golden, orange dashi. Pour your dashi into a lidded donabe pot and keep warm.

Chef's Tip

The sublime kombu-infused dashi, steeped in tomato liquor, gives this dish a mesmerising colour and flavour. Fresh samphire, scallop and herbs make it scintillatingly fresh. The preparation for this can take up to a day.

For The Shiitake Mushrooms

Cover the shiitake mushrooms with rice wine vinegar, season with a little soy sauce and a few splashes of mirin. Leave to pickle and set aside.

For The Scallops

Slice through the scallops so they are half the thickness. Add the rapeseed oil to a hot pan and cook for 60-70 seconds on each side. Season, then place on a cloth for a minute to rest.

To Serve

Sprinkle sea herbs, such as sea beet, ice lettuce and sea buckthorn into your dashi, as well as samphire. Put the scallops into the pot, then add a teaspoon of the caviar of your choice. Garnish with nasturtium flowers and season with droplets of chilli shrimp oil.

CLAMS & HAM

Havana Republic

18 Abbey Foregate, Shrewsbury, Shropshire, SY2 6AE

01743 281 744 www.havanarepublic.co.uk Twitter: @HavanaRepublic1

SERVES 4

Tumul Flats Pinot Noir (New Zealand) or Morgon, Côte de Py, Domaine de la Chaponne, Laurent Guillet Beaujolais 2014 (France)

Ingredients

Clams And Ham

8 razor clams

24 normal clams

rapeseed oil (to fry)

4 cloves garlic

8 shallots (finely chopped)

4 tomatoes (skinned, cored, diced)

butter (knob of)

200g chorizo (cut into 5mm dice)

600g precooked black-eyed beans

4 tsp XO sauce

1 small bird's eye chilli (finely diced)

12 leaves cavolo nero

To Serve

micro herbs

Method

For The Clams And Ham

Spray the razor clams liberally with rapeseed oil, then pop them under the grill.

The clams will start to open and when they do, take them out. They should take 1½–2 minutes under a 160°C grill. Remove the gut sac and discard. Trim the clams, cut into 3 and place to one side.

Fry the garlic and shallots in a little rapeseed oil. Add the diced tomato. Now add a little butter and throw in your chorizo dice. Once they start to go brown, add the black-eyed beans. Don't be afraid to give it plenty of vigorous heat.

Throw in your regular clams, turn down the heat and put a saucepan lid on top, to keep in the steam. This will help to cook the clams and their shells will start to open. Discard any that don't open.

When the clams are open, the dish is ready to be seasoned. Add the XO sauce and bird's eye chilli, then mix in the cavolo nero leaves. To finish, add the razor clam meat.

Chef's Tip

There is a myriad of versions of surf and turf and this one's a real belter. Razor clams are an underused ingredient, though I think they're delicious. They have a scallop-like texture and a sweet-salty flavour. The addition of salty ham provides a perfect counterpoint.

To Serve

Clean the razor clam shells, then gently spoon the mix into them. Add the remaining clams to the plate and spoon the black-eyed beans around. Garnish with micro herbs.

THE ISLAND

The Peach Tree
18 Abbey Foregate, Shrewsbury, Shropshire, SY2 6AE
01743 355 055 www.thepeachtree.co.uk Twitter: @ThePeachTree1

SERVES 4

Mas Amiel Maury 2010
(France)

Ingredients

Caramel

90ml double cream
28g butter
24g honey
24ml water
80g caster sugar

Chocolate Nemesis

270g dark chocolate
180g unsalted butter
4 eggs
270g caster sugar

To Serve

good quality vanilla ice cream
fresh mint
edible viola flowers
chocolate soil
pulled caramel (shards of)
strawberries (optional)

Method

For The Caramel

Heat the cream and butter until they are fully incorporated. Boil the honey and water with the sugar, then add the cream mix. Boil for about 10 minutes to 120°C.

For The Chocolate Nemesis

Preheat the oven to 120°C (fan).

Melt the dark chocolate and butter, then add the caramel to the chocolate mix. Whisk the eggs and sugar for 10 minutes and fold the chocolate mix into the eggs. Put into a tray and bake for 1 hour.

To Serve

Place a ball of ice cream in each bowl. Spoon the caramel chocolate nemesis over the top and decorate with chocolate soil, mint, edible flowers and other garnishes. You could also use fruit - strawberries work a treat.

Chef's Tip

There are various methods for making chocolate soil, the easiest of which is to take a packet of Minstrels and blitz them at a high speed in a food processor!

168
THE PLOUGH INN

Cleobury Road, Far Forest, Kidderminster, DY14 9TE

01299 266 237
www.theploughinn.org Facebook: The Plough Inn

The Plough Inn, owned by the Giles family since 2001, is a very popular eatery situated in the north of Worcestershire overlooking one of England's most ancient forests.

As well as offering a diverse à la carte menu, The Plough Inn is home of the AGA Carvery, renowned as one of the best in the country. The talented chefs travel to Birmingham market weekly with the emphasis on sourcing the freshest, highest quality produce locally, which has helped the carvery earn such a fantastic reputation.

The country inn offers a range of facilities such as outside catering, hog roasts, a Mediterranean style bar and a beer garden, where during the summer months, customers can enjoy the fresh air with a relaxing drink, choosing from the wide range of real ales and wines on offer.

The interior has undergone an extensive renovation where attention to detail has been meticulous. There is a unique, hand-painted glass conservatory with award-winning toilets where pictures of local sights adorn the walls.

Following on from the success of their winning formula in 2005, the business expanded acquiring a second site, 'Ye Olde Punch Bowl Inn' and from there, Nostalgia Inns was born.

The chefs, Ben Giles and Edward Link, locally source fresh ingredients to create modern, British food with an artistic flair. "We believe in simple food done the proper way, which returns us custom time and time again." Ben Giles.

FIVE SPICE DUCK RILLETTE, SESAME PRAWN TOAST, PLUM PURÉE

SERVES 4

Piesporter Michelsberg, Mosel (Germany)

Ingredients

Five Spice Duck Rillette

2 duck legs
4g Chinese five spice (plus extra to taste)
2 star anise
4 black peppercorns
1 clove garlic
500g duck fat

Sesame Prawn Toast

100g prawns (cooked, peeled)
12g root ginger (grated)
2 spring onions
1 egg white
20ml light soy sauce
40g cornflour
seasoning
2 slices bread
100g sesame seeds
sesame oil (to fry)

Plum Purée

6 Victoria plums
100g caster sugar
50ml water
3g malic acid

Garnish

2 Victoria plums (halved and poached)
micro herbs

Method

For The Five Spice Duck Rillette (Allow 48 hours)

Preheat the oven to 92°C (fan).

Season the duck legs with the Chinese five spice, add the rest of the ingredients and cover with duck fat. *Confit* in the oven for 12 hours.

Allow to cool, strip the meat off the legs and blitz with just enough *confit* oil to bind. Season again with Chinese five spice, as desired, to taste.

Ballotine the duck in cling film. Leave to set in the fridge for at least 4 hours, or ideally overnight. Remove the cling film and cut into 4 pieces when ready to serve.

> **Chef's Tip**
>
> You can store the duck legs in *confit* for up to 1 month after cooking them.

For The Sesame Prawn Toast

Blitz the prawns, ginger, spring onions, egg white, soy sauce and cornflour to a paste, then season.

Spread one side of each slice of bread with the prawn paste and cover with sesame seeds. Pan fry the bread in sesame oil on each side until cooked. Cut into desired shape.

For The Plum Purée

Destone the plums and place them in a heavy bottomed pan. Add the sugar and water and simmer until soft. Blitz until smooth, finally stirring in the malic acid.

To Serve

Serve as pictured.

(see glossary)

ASSIETTE OF SPRING LAMB

SERVES 4

Clos du Mont-Olivet, Châteauneuf-du-Pape (France)

Ingredients

Lamb Loin
1 lamb loin
seasoning, 50g butter
2 sprigs thyme

Lamb Neck Tortellini Filling
1 lamb neck
300g mirepoix (carrot, celery, onion, leek, bay leaf, thyme, peppercorn)
2 bay leaves, 200ml red wine

Pasta Dough For The Tortellini
250g pasta 00 flour
2 small eggs, 1 egg yolk
30ml water
10ml olive oil

Croquettes
1 large Maris Piper potato (peeled)
1 cooking onion
1 clove garlic
200g lean lamb mince
50ml veal stock
50g Parmesan
30g frozen peas
egg, flour, breadcrumbs (to *pane*)

Wild Garlic Purée
1 cauliflower
500g wild garlic
250g butter, seasoning

Pearl Barley
200g pearl barley
50g butter
1 onion (chopped)
2 cloves garlic (chopped)
300ml brown chicken stock
50g wild garlic purée

To Garnish And Serve
wild garlic flowers
baby vegetables
lamb jus

Method

For The Lamb Loin
Cut the lamb loin into 4 and season. Vac pack individually and place into a water bath at 56°C for 35 minutes. Place the lamb and thyme in a pan, basting with butter until golden brown. Leave to rest for 3 minutes. Alternatively, colour in a hot pan, then place in the oven for 6 minutes at 180°C (fan).

For The Lamb Neck Tortellini
Preheat the oven to 125°C (fan).

Brown the lamb neck in a pan, then set aside. In the same pan, sauté the mirepoix until soft, then deglaze with red wine. Return the neck to the pan with the bay leaves and braise for 3 hours in the oven.

Flake the meat into a bowl. Reduce the cooking liquor, then stir in the flaked meat. Season to taste.

Place all the pasta dough ingredients into a processor and pulse together to form a dough. Wrap in cling film and rest in the fridge for 30 minutes. Roll the dough out on a pasta machine to number 2.

Cut the pasta dough into discs, place a little of the lamb neck filling in the middle. Fold over and seal with water. Wrap around your finger to form tortellini. Cook the tortellini in a pan of boiling, salted water for 2 minutes when ready to serve.

For The Croquettes
Steam the potato until soft, mash and leave to cool. Sauté the onion and garlic until soft, then brown the lamb mince. Add the veal stock and slowly braise for 1 hour, or until reduced.

Add the Parmesan and peas, season to taste. Mix in the potato, roll into 75g cylinders and *pane*. Deep fry for 3-4 minutes until golden.

For The Wild Garlic Purée
Wilt the wild garlic and refresh in cold water. Boil the cauliflower until tender and strain.

Place all the ingredients into a Thermomix and blitz for 5 minutes until silky smooth. Alternatively, blitz in a food processor, then pass through a *chinois*.

> **Chef's Tip**
> The wild garlic season is from March to May. It normally grows by the water's edge and is a very versatile, foraged ingredient.

For The Pearl Barley
Sauté the onions and garlic in butter until soft. Add the barley and cook with the chicken stock, adding a little at a time until the barley is soft. Fold through the wild garlic purée and season to taste.

To Serve
Serve as pictured.

TEXTURES OF BLOOD ORANGE

SERVES 6

🍷 *Prosecco*
(Italy)

Ingredients

Blood Orange Jelly

480ml Boiron blood orange purée
2g malic acid
50g caster sugar
4 sheets gelatine (softened in water)

Blood Orange Sorbet

100ml water
100g caster sugar
200ml Boiron blood orange purée
20g egg whites

Macarons

75g ground almonds
75g icing sugar
2 egg whites (keep separate)
2g orange colour powder
1 drop orange essence
80g caster sugar
40ml water

Semi Gel

100ml Boiron blood orange purée
25g caster sugar
12g ultratex
1g malic acid

Garnish

blood orange jus pipette (optional)
basil leaves
sugar twist
pistachios (crushed)
freeze dried citrus fruit (lemon and orange)

20cm square tin (lined with cling film)

Method

For The Blood Orange Jelly (Prepare ahead)

Heat the orange purée, malic acid and sugar to 80°C. Stir in the gelatine until melted, then pour into the prepared tin. Leave to set in the fridge for 4 hours, or preferably overnight. Cut into long strips when ready to serve.

For The Blood Orange Sorbet (Prepare ahead)

Bring the water and sugar to the boil to create a syrup. Combine the stock syrup and blood orange purée together, then leave to cool. Once cooled, mix in the egg whites and churn in an ice cream machine. Freeze overnight or until ready to use.

For The Macarons

Place the almonds, icing sugar, 1 egg white, orange powder and essence in a processor. Pulse to a paste and set aside.

Bring the water and sugar up to 120°C. Start whisking the remaining egg white in a Kitchen Aid, then slowly pour the stock syrup into the egg white, whisking continuously to form a meringue.

Fold the meringue through the almond paste and spoon the mixture into a piping bag. Pipe 2cm rounds on a baking mat.

Preheat the oven to 160°C (fan).

Leave the piped mixture at room temperature for 30 minutes to form a slight crust. Bake in the oven for 14 minutes, remove and leave to cool completely.

For The Semi Gel

Gently heat the blood orange purée and season with sugar to taste. Whisk in the ultratex and malic acid to reach your preferred consistency.

To Serve

Sandwich the macaron halves together using the semi gel and serve as pictured.

> **Chef's Tip**
>
> If you can't source Boiron blood orange purée, use the freshly squeezed juice from blood oranges. When choosing blood oranges at the market, always look for red tinted oranges which usually indicates a red orange flesh.

178
THE POUND INN

Leebotwood, Near Church Stretton, Shropshire, SY6 6ND

01694 751 477
www.thepound.org.uk Twitter: @PoundInn

The Pound Inn at Leebotwood is a 15th Century thatched country pub and restaurant, run by Neil and Sarah McCann along with chef Harry Bullock. The Pound Inn is situated in the heart of the Shropshire Marches between Shrewsbury and Church Stretton. Built circa 1457 and founded as a drovers' hostelry, the building became an Inn in 1823 when the former Pound Inn was burnt down.

Working side by side, Neil and Harry share a passion for classic dishes with a modern twist, using fresh, seasonal, local and, where possible, home grown produce. Their menu champions pub classics alongside an à la carte menu of dishes which push the boundary.

Originally from Northern Ireland, Neil has been a chef for over 20 years, working in, and achieving awards for restaurants in his home - County Down. After working throughout the UK, Neil came to Shropshire and took the role as Claude Bosi's head chef at The Bell at Yarpole, before taking on The Pound with his wife Sarah.

Still just 18 years old, Harry Bullock, a vastly self-taught chef, started his career at La Bécasse at the age of 13. Passion and determination has led him to develop a unique relationship with food, connecting with the ingredients and even growing them in his kitchen garden. This young chef has certainly set himself a bright future.

The Pound Inn aims to deliver consistent quality dishes with fresh, seasonal and locally sourced produce, supported by a friendly and efficient front of house team, creating an environment that can be enjoyed for any occasion.

TASTE OF FRESH CRAB, AVOCADO, PINK GRAPEFRUIT & APPLE

SERVES 4

Chablis 'Pierrelee' La Chablisienne
(Burgundy, France)

Ingredients

Dressed White Crabmeat

1 live male crab (white meat of)
25g crème fraîche
20g apple (finely *brunoise*)
5g dill fronds (chopped)
lemon juice (to taste)
salt and pepper

Bisque Gel

roasted crab shells
2 banana shallots
4 cloves garlic
1 bay leaf
5g thyme
parsley stalks (small bunch of)
50ml olive oil
4 carrots
2 sticks celery
½ bulb fennel
1 red pepper
25ml Pernod
4 vine tomatoes
4g agar agar

Avocado Purée And Pink Grapefruit

1 ripe avocado
50g crème fraîche
lemon juice (splash of)
salt and pepper
1 pink grapefruit

Garnish

1 Granny Smith apple (*julienne*)
garden radish (sliced thinly)
borage shoots
dill fronds

Additional Components

brown crab pangrattato
brown crab crisp

Method

To Prepare And Cook The Crab

Place the crab in the refrigerator, covered with a damp tea towel, for at least half an hour; this will make the crab slightly dozy and unaware. Remove from the fridge and place upside-down on a metal tray. Using a clean screwdriver, lift the flap on the underside of the crab and pierce a hole with the screwdriver very quickly; this will instantly kill the crab. Bring a large pan of water to the boil and season with salt, add the crab and cook for 15 minutes per kilogram. When cooked, remove the crab and let it cool naturally. Refrigerate.

Chef's Tip

Always cook the crab within minutes of killing it; if you leave it, the bacteria will multiply rapidly and it will be unsafe to eat.

For The Bisque Gel

Roughly chop all the vegetables. Heat the oil in a large stock pan, add the shallots, garlic and herbs, lightly sauté, then add the carrots, celery, fennel and red pepper, and fry until softened. Add the Pernod and flambé. Stir in the tomatoes to create a light ragout. Once the tomatoes have broken down, add the crab shells and cover with water. Simmer for 3 hours. Pick out the shells and blend the sauce until all of the vegetable pulp is incorporated, then pass through a *chinois*. Reduce the bisque to 500ml, season, then pass through a muslin cloth to remove any further impurities. Bring to the boil and add the agar agar. Refrigerate for 1 hour, then blitz to create a gel.

For The Avocado Purée And Pink Grapefruit

Reserve half the avocado for use as a garnish. Blitz the other half with the crème fraîche and lemon juice to create a stiff purée. Season to taste. Remove the peel from the grapefruit with a sharp knife, then segment.

To Assemble

Dress the crab, then pick through the white meat to remove any shell. Mix with the crème fraîche, apple, dill and lemon juice, and season to taste. Divide the crab between your plates and garnish with all of the components as shown.

SHROPSHIRE LAMB, GOOSEBERRIES, LEMON THYME POMMES ANNA

SERVES 4

🍷 *Yarra Valley Pinot Noir, Robert Oatley (Australia)*

Ingredients

1 x 4 bone rack of lamb (*French trimmed*)
230g lamb fillet (seasoned), 60g butter

Lamb Belly

1 lamb belly (bone in), 200g salt
2 sprigs thyme (1 chopped, 1 whole)
2 sprigs rosemary (1 chopped, 1 whole)
1 shallot (chopped), 1 carrot (chopped)
1 stick celery (chopped)
2 cloves garlic (chopped), 2 bay leaves
500ml lamb stock
110g plain flour (seasoned)
2 eggs (well beaten), 170g breadcrumbs

Lemon Thyme Pommes Anna

8 large potatoes (sliced very thinly on a mandolin)
125g butter (melted)
salt and pepper
2 sprigs lemon thyme (chopped)

Gooseberry Purée

280g gooseberries, 30ml water
salt (pinch of), sugar (pinch of)
1 sprig rosemary

Pea Purée

280g fresh peas, ½ shallot (finely chopped)
oil (for frying), salt and pepper (to taste)
250ml chicken stock

To Serve

1 bunch heritage carrots
1 bunch heritage candy beetroot
8 runner beans (topped and tailed), 1 courgette

terrine mould (lined with greaseproof paper, buttered)

> **Chef's Tip**
> Ask your butcher to score and *French trim* your lamb rack and trim all fat off the lamb fillet.

Method

For The Lamb Belly (Allow 40 hours)
Rub the lamb belly with salt, chopped thyme and chopped rosemary. Cover with cling film and refrigerate overnight. Preheat the oven to 120ºC (fan).

Wash the belly under cold water and dry well. Fry on both sides in oil in a large roasting tin until golden. Add the vegetables and herbs, pour in the stock, cover with foil and cook for 4 hours.

Remove the belly from the stock and place on a tray to cool slightly. Remove all the meat from the belly, discarding any bones and fat. Place the lamb belly meat in the centre of a large square of cling film, then roll into a sausage making sure all the air is removed. Repeat the step twice, tie both ends and refrigerate overnight. Slice into portions and *pane*.

Pass the cooking liquor through a sieve and refrigerate. Once cold, remove the fat, then pass through a sieve again into a pan. Place on a high heat and reduce by a third. Reheat for serving.

For The Lemon Thyme Pommes Anna (Prepare the day before)
Preheat the oven to 180ºC (fan).

Fill the terrine mould with layers of potato, seasoned and brushed with butter, until all are used. Cover with foil and bake for 30 minutes. Remove foil and cook for 10 minutes. Cool slightly, cover with greaseproof paper, then press with a heavy weight overnight in the fridge.

For The Gooseberry Purée
Boil the ingredients for 2 minutes, discard the rosemary, then blitz to a purée. Pass through a sieve.

For The Pea Purée
Fry the shallot in oil (medium heat) for 1 minute. Add the peas, fry for 1 minute, then simmer with the stock for 2 minutes. Blitz to a purée, pass through a sieve and season to taste.

To Assemble
Preheat the oven to 180ºC (fan).

Oil and season the lamb rack and fry, skin-side down, for 1 minute in a large pan. Sear all over and baste with 30g butter. Place in the oven for 25 minutes for medium.

Slice the Pommes Anna in 4. Fry the slices on a medium heat for 1 minute on each side until golden. Place in the oven for 10 minutes.

Caramelise the lamb fillet over a medium heat, add 30g butter and baste for 3-4 minutes.

Remove the rack from the oven and place onto a tray with the fillet. Cover with foil and leave to rest.

Deep fry the lamb belly slices in oil (180ºC) for 4 minutes until golden brown. Drain on kitchen paper. Assemble as pictured.

LOGANBERRY SEMIFREDDO, DARK CHOCOLATE & LOGANBERRY TEXTURES

SERVES 4

*Aroha Bay Marlborough Sauvignon Blanc
(New Zealand)
With classically intense gooseberry flavours and a
clean lingering finish, this is a popular white from
New Zealand's premium Marlborough region.*

Ingredients

Loganberry Semifreddo

200g loganberry purée
8 egg yolks
200g caster sugar
300ml double cream (semi-whipped)

Whipped Chocolate Ganache

300g 70% dark chocolate
200ml full-fat milk
150ml double cream
40g unsalted butter

Loganberry Purée

300g fresh loganberries (stalks removed)
25g caster sugar
25ml water

Chocolate And Loganberry Meringue

3 egg whites
150g caster sugar
10g 70% dark chocolate (blitzed)
5g dehydrated loganberries

Chocolate Soil

75g caster sugar
25ml water
80g 70% dark chocolate

Additional Components

fresh loganberries
dehydrated loganberries

4 tube moulds

Method

For The Loganberry Semifreddo

Whisk the egg yolks and the sugar together until light and airy.
It should leave a trail when the whisk is lifted. Fold in the
loganberry purée, followed by the double cream. Pour into tube
moulds and freeze for at least 4 hours.

For The Whipped Chocolate Ganache

Place the chocolate into a metal bowl. Bring the milk and cream
just to the boil in a solid based pan. Pour the hot cream over
the chocolate and stir gently. Once amalgamated, add the butter
in small cubes whilst continuing to mix. Chill for 4 hours until
set. Place the ganache in a Kitchen Aid and whip with the 'K'
beater until the colour of the ganache becomes light and the
texture airy. Place in a piping bag and refrigerate until needed.

For The Loganberry Purée

Place all the ingredients into a solid based pan and bring to a
gentle simmer. Cook for 20 minutes. Transfer the mix into a
food processor and blend on high for 3 minutes. Pass the purée
through a *chinois* and chill.

For The Chocolate And Loganberry Meringue

Preheat the oven to 60ºC (fan).

Whisk the egg whites to stiff peak. Slowly start adding the
sugar, 1 teaspoon at a time. Once all of the sugar has been
added, stop whisking. Spread the meringue thinly on a flat tray
lined with baking parchment and sprinkle with the chocolate
and dehydrated loganberries. Bake until fully crisp,
approximately 3 hours.

For The Chocolate Soil

Bring the water and sugar to 110ºC in a pan. Add the chocolate
and whisk for 30 seconds. The consistency will change to a
grainy, soil-like texture. Remove from the pan and allow to cool
on a tray.

To Assemble

Remove the semifreddo from the moulds, roll in a little
dehydrated loganberry and stand up on the plate. Pipe on the
ganache, spot some purée around the plate and stand some
shards of the meringue against the semifreddo. Garnish with a
little fresh loganberry and the chocolate soil.

Chef's Tip

Other berries such as raspberries and blackberries will work
well if loganberries can't be sourced.

188
RESTAURANT 23

34 Hamilton Terrace, Leamington Spa, Warwickshire, CV32 4LY

01926 422 422
www.restaurant23.co.uk Twitter: @restaurant23 @peterknibb

A warm welcome is always on offer at Restaurant 23 and Morgan's Bar.

They desire to give guests a unique, highly satisfying and relaxed fine dining experience. Not only does this mean they aim to serve the finest local ingredients, cooked to perfection in innovative and exciting dishes in the restaurant, but in their cocktail bar, they have created an ideal environment for guests to relax and unwind. With every element - from dishes to décor, cocktails to service - they want to make your fine dining experience fantastic, and one to remember.

Peter Knibb, head chef/proprietor was born and brought up locally. He studied at The Trinity School and trained at Stratford College before completing a work placement at Claridge's Hotel in London.

Following his placement, he was invited to join the team, working under head chef John Williams. Here, Peter discovered his cooking direction and set off to gain further knowledge and experience of modern European cuisine.

This led him to work under Paul Rhodes in the 3 Michelin starred Chez Nico, as well as stints as chef on board the luxury yacht 'Seaborne Goddess' (catering for Cliff Richard's 60th birthday party among others) and the Gucci family's private yacht as it cruised the Mediterranean and the Caribbean.

Peter's travels then took him to the Michelin starred Mallory Court Hotel and also to work as a sous chef under Jun Tanaka in the Pearl Restaurant in London, before opening the doors to his own restaurant in May 2006. Restaurant 23 has gone from strength to strength, gaining 3 AA Rosettes in the 2013/14 guide.

Located in a grand white Victorian building in the centre of Leamington Spa, Restaurant 23 has gained various awards including 3 AA Rosettes. It is recommended in the Michelin Guide and also The Good Food Guide.

CHAMPAGNE

Laurent-Perrier

MAISON FONDÉE 1812

ROASTED QUAIL, CONFIT LEG PASTILLA, FIG PUREE, PISTACHIO

SERVES 4

Radford Dale 'Freedom' Pinot Noir 2012
(South Africa)

Ingredients

Quail

4 medium quails (legs and wings removed)
salt and black pepper
3 cloves garlic (2 chopped, 1 whole)
2 sprigs thyme (2 picked, 1 whole)
duck fat (to cover)
50g butter

Confit Leg Pastilla

50g couscous
olive oil
½ small onion (finely chopped)
1 clove garlic (finely chopped)
30g sultanas
½ tsp ground turmeric
½ tsp cumin seeds
½ tsp ground cinnamon
125g confit quail leg meat
30g feta cheese (crumbled)
fresh coriander (to taste, chopped)
1 lemon (zest and juice of)
2 sheets feuille de brick or spring roll pastry
1 egg white and 30g plain flour (mixed to a paste or 'glue')

Fig Purée

4 fresh figs
75ml port
75ml red wine
50g sugar
lemon juice (to taste)
¼ stick cinnamon

Garnish

1 fig
1 tbsp Iranian pistachios (chopped)
coriander cress

Method

To Prepare The Quail

Remove the wishbone from the quail crown and reserve in the fridge.

Rub the legs with salt, black pepper, chopped garlic and picked thyme and leave for 2 hours. Wash off and *confit* in duck fat for about 30-40 minutes over a very low heat. Remove from the fat and cool, then pick the meat from the bones and skin.

For The Confit Leg Pastilla

Place the couscous in a bowl, drizzle with olive oil, season with salt and mix well. Pour in 50ml of boiling water, cling film the bowl and leave for 10 minutes.

Sauté the onion, garlic and sultanas in a little olive oil along with the turmeric, cinnamon and cumin seeds for 15 minutes, or until softened, stirring occasionally. Remove from the heat and add the picked quail leg meat. Stir the quail mixture into the couscous, then the crumbled feta, chopped coriander, lemon juice and zest.

Cut the pastry sheets in half and trim the side to form a triangle. Lay the couscous mix along the shortest edge of each sheet. Roll each one up halfway, fold in the sides, then continue rolling up like big cigars. Wet the joins with the flour and egg white 'glue'. Leave to set for 10 minutes.

For The Fig Purée

Simmer everything together for 20-30 minutes; the liquid should be slightly reduced so you have a nice glossy purée. Blitz the figs in a blender then pass through a sieve. Reduce over a low heat if the purée is too thin.

Chef's Tip

Turkish figs are the best for this dish and at their best from September to November.

To Serve

Preheat the oven to 180°C.

Sear the quail on either side of the breast, then place on its back. Add the butter, garlic clove and the thyme. Roast in the oven for 5 minutes, baste the quail, then return to the oven for a further 5 minutes. Baste again and leave to rest for 10 minutes. Carve the breasts away from the bone and keep warm. Deep fry the pastilla until crispy, then cut in half. Serve as pictured.

ROASTED MONKFISH, BBQ RED PEPPERS, ROASTED LEMON PUREE, CUMBRIAN HAM

SERVES 4

🍷 *Chablis Domaine Garnier & Fils 2013 (France)*

Ingredients

Monkfish

400-500g monkfish fillet (cut into 12 even pieces)
50ml extra virgin olive oil
40g butter
1 lemon (segmented)
10g capers
1 tbsp dill (chopped)
1 tbsp tarragon (chopped)

BBQ Red Peppers

2 red peppers
olive oil
salt
2 shallots (chopped)

Roasted Lemon Purée

2 unwaxed lemons
5g sea salt
5ml lemon juice
5ml orange juice
1 clove garlic (crushed)
125ml olive oil

Garnish

confit potatoes cooked in pomace olive oil, garlic and salt
sea vegetables (sea aster, sea purslane, samphire)
3 slices Woodall's Cumbrian ham

Method

To Prepare The Monkish

Trim the monkfish, salt it for 30 minutes, then wash off and pat dry.

> **Chef's Tip**
> Pre-order your fish at the fishmonger to get the freshest fish possible.

For The BBQ Red Peppers

Roll the peppers in olive oil and salt, then BBQ, grill or griddle until blackened. Place in a bowl, cover with cling film and leave to cool. When cool, peel off the skin and discard. Cut the peppers into neat triangles and set aside. Sweat the shallots and any pepper trimmings, then purée, pass through a sieve and keep warm.

For The Roasted Lemon Purée

Preheat the oven to 180°C.

Roast the lemons on the salt in foil until soft, about 30 minutes.

Scoop out the flesh of the lemon into a bowl, then scrape away the pith from the skin. Discard the pith and chop the skin. Place all the ingredients, except the oil, in a blender with a little water and blend for 2 minutes, then add the oil to *emulsify*. Blend on full power for a further 4 minutes, then pass through a sieve.

To Assemble The Dish

Roast the monkfish in a hot pan with olive oil, getting a good amount of colour on the cut side. Add the butter, then turn the fish over. Baste with the butter for a further 2 minutes, then leave to rest in a warm place for 5 minutes. Remove the fish from the pan. Add the lemon segments, capers and herbs to the cooking juices and set aside.

Blanch the sea vegetables, warm the ingredients through and arrange on the plate in a neat circle. Finish with the pan juices, pureés and Cumbrian ham.

CHOCOLATE GANACHE, RASPBERRIES, GOAT'S MILK SORBET

SERVES 8

Late Bottled Vintage Port, Quinta Do Crasto, 2008 (Portugal)

Ingredients

Raspberry And Pistachio Macaron
First Stage:
75g ground almonds
75g icing sugar
25g egg white

Second Stage:
75g caster sugar
25g water
30g egg whites
red and green food colour (a few drops of)
pistachio paste (to taste)
50g butter (softened)
icing sugar (to taste)
raspberry gel (to sandwich)

Goat's Milk Sorbet
290ml water
240g sugar
400ml goat's milk
100g Greek yoghurt
70ml lemon juice
50g glucose

Base
100g cornflakes
200g hazelnut praline paste

Chocolate Ganache
400ml double cream
50g trimoline
450g Valrhona Manjari chocolate 64%
65g butter

Garnish
32 fresh raspberries
Iranian pistachios (chopped)
raspberry gel
chocolate soil

small metal rectangular mould

Method

For The Raspberry And Pistachio Macaron

Mix together the first stage ingredients to form a paste.

For the second stage, boil the sugar and water to 118°C. Whisk the egg whites to soft peaks, then add the hot sugar mix and continue to whisk until cool. Fold the meringue into the almond paste in 3 stages.

Add the red food colouring to half of the mix and the green colouring to the other half. Transfer into 2 piping bags. Pipe the mix onto baking paper to form 2½cm discs. Leave the paste to form a skin, then bake in the oven at 130°C for 15 minutes. Leave to cool.

Whip the butter with a little icing sugar until light in colour. Add the pistachio paste to taste.

Fill the macarons with the butter cream and a little raspberry gel using one red and one green macaron.

For The Goat's Milk Sorbet

Bring all the ingredients to the boil, then place into a bowl to cool down. Chill in the fridge for 1 hour, then churn in an ice cream machine and freeze.

For The Base

Blend the praline paste and cornflakes in a blender until well combined. Place into the mould (½ cm thick) and set in the fridge for 1 hour.

To Make The Ganache

Boil the cream and trimoline and reduce down to 375ml. Add the chocolate, in 3 stages while stirring, then add the butter and blend until smooth and glossy. Pour onto the base and set in the fridge for 4 hours.

To Serve

Heat the metal mould with a blow torch to release the chocolate ganache and base. Cut into strips, 1cm by 9cm.

Carefully place the ganache on top of the raspberry gel. Sit a macaron on top of the chopped pistachios and a *quenelle* of sorbet on top of the chocolate soil. Garnish with 4 fresh raspberries per person.

Chef's Tip
Use a hot knife when cutting the chocolate ganache, and blow torch for one second to get a nice shine on the chocolate.

198
SIMPSONS
RESTAURANT

20 Highfield Road, Edgbaston, Birmingham, B15 3DU

0121 454 3434
www.simpsonsrestaurant.co.uk Twitter: @simpsons_rest

Simpsons Restaurant in Edgbaston raised the standard of dining in Birmingham 11 years ago and has maintained its position as best in the city ever since.

Chef director Luke Tipping has been in the kitchen for the past 21 years. Originating from the 'Simpsons' restaurant, he was partnered with Andreas Antona, in Kenilworth, Warwickshire. The restaurant moved to Edgbaston back in 2003, having been awarded a Michelin star status in the year 2000; a rank which it still maintains today.

At Simpsons, only the finest ingredients will do - transformed so that they may produce perfectly balanced, flavourful dishes by Luke and his talented team. A frequently changing menu celebrates the very best of what's in season, only made better through the guidance of Luke's expert hand and his natural, yet attentive cooking style.

There is a cookery school for those wishing to improve their own culinary skills - so popular that it's booked out months in advance.

Whilst the ambience at Simpsons has always been friendly rather than formal, its recent refurbishment has brought a modern, fresh look and a more casual dining experience.

Depending on the time of year, dishes can be enjoyed in the main dining room where natural light shines through the ceiling and patio doors, or in the restaurant's beautifully appointed al fresco space - an oasis of calm just five minutes drive from the city centre.

Simpsons has held a Michelin star since 2000, as well as having being awarded a 3 AA Rosette. Many of the kitchen team, past and present, have received recognition for their skills and dedication through various competitions around the Midlands.

CITRUS CURED SALMON, FROZEN HORSERADISH, CUCUMBER KETCHUP

SERVES 4

🍷 *Wild Sauvignon Greywacke, Marlborough, 2013 (New Zealand)*

Ingredients

Citrus Cured Salmon

300g organic salmon
1 pink grapefruit (peeled, pith removed)
1 orange (peeled, pith removed)
80g course sea salt
120g granulated sugar
6g juniper berries (chopped)
½ bunch dill (chopped)

Cucumber Ketchup

1 cucumber (peeled, deseeded)
20g ultratex
salt (to season)
sugar (to season)
white wine vinegar (dash of)

Frozen Horseradish

90ml milk
15g cornflour
500ml buttermilk
75g horseradish (peeled, grated)

Horseradish Mayonnaise

100g mayonnaise
20g horseradish (peeled, finely grated)
lemon (squeeze of)

Compressed Cucumber

1 cucumber (peeled, deseeded)
white balsamic vinegar (a few drops of)

Garnish

nasturtium leaves
dill
salmon keta

Method

For The Citrus Cured Salmon (Prepare at least a day in advance)
Cut 4 segments from the grapefruit and orange and reserve for the garnish. Slice the rest of the fruit thinly and set aside.
Combine the salt, sugar, juniper berries and dill. Place a large sheet of cling film on a stainless steel or glass tray and lay half the fruit slices in the same shape as the salmon on the cling film.
Sprinkle with half of the salt, place the salmon on the fruit, cover with the remaining salt and top with the rest of the citrus fruit.
Wrap the salmon in the cling film and refrigerate for 18-24 hours. You can tell when the salmon is ready when it is firm and the texture even.
Discard the marinade, rinse the salmon in cold water, pat dry and wrap in fresh cling film. Chill for a further 4-6 hours.

Chef's Tip
This could work as well with a good quality smoked salmon rather than citrus cured.

For The Cucumber Ketchup
Blend the cucumber on a high speed in a food processor, then add the ultratex until it becomes a thick consistency. Season with salt, sugar and a dash of vinegar. Store in a squeezy bottle until ready to use.

For The Frozen Horseradish (Prepare 24 hours ahead)
Bring the milk to the boil, add the cornflour and stir until thickened. Remove from the heat and stir in the buttermilk and horseradish. Leave to cool. Pour the mixture into a suitable container, cover the surface with cling film and freeze overnight.
When ready to use, remove from the freezer and, using a fork, carefully scrape the top off the mixture to create fine ice. Store the remainder in the freezer.

For The Horseradish Mayonnaise
Combine the mayonnaise and horseradish. Squeeze in lemon juice to taste. Set aside.

For The Compressed Cucumber
Cut the cucumber into pieces and place in a vac pack bag with a few drops of vinegar. Seal on high in a vacuum pack machine. Leave in the bag until ready to serve.

To Assemble The Dish
Place a spoonful of horseradish mayonnaise onto a plate and spread with the back of the spoon. Cut the salmon into 4 portions and place on top of the mayonnaise. Arrange the cucumber around the salmon and dot with the ketchup. Scatter nasturtium leaves, dill and salmon keta over the salmon. Finish with a sprinkling of the frozen horseradish.

BELLY OF LAMB, RADISH, FETA CHEESE, GREEN BEANS, CHICKPEA PUREE, LOVAGE

SERVES 4

Petit Verdot Remolinos Vineyard, Finca Decero, Mendoza, 2011 (Argentina)

Ingredients

Lamb

2 lamb bellies (trimmed of excess fat)
meat glue (to dust)
salt and pepper (to season)
flour (to dust)
vegetable oil (dash of)

Chickpea Purée

200g chickpeas (cooked)
50ml olive oil
1 tsp garlic (chopped)
salt (to season)
ground cumin (pinch of)
50ml natural yoghurt

Lamb Jus

2kg lamb bones and trim (chopped)
1 carrot
½ onion
1 stick celery (peeled, finely chopped)
2½ litres water (to cover)
5g butter

To Serve

200g green beans (trimmed)
butter (knob of)
75g feta cheese (diced)
1 tbsp lovage (chopped)
chickpeas (handful of, cooked)

Garnish

2 radishes (halved)

Method

To Prepare And Cook The Lamb (Prepare ahead)

Place the bellies onto several layers of cling film. Dust with meat glue and season with salt and pepper. Roll them into a cylinder as tightly as you can and seal at both ends. Reserve in the fridge overnight.

Preheat the oven to 80°C (steam setting).

Roll the lamb in foil, then place in the oven and cook for 12 hours. Carefully remove from the oven, remove the foil and cling film and slice into 4 equal portions, then dust with flour. Place on a clean tray and cool in the fridge overnight. Alternatively, cook the lamb *sous vide* in a water bath at 75°C for 12 hours.

Heat a non-stick pan on a medium heat and add a dash of vegetable oil. Carefully place the lamb into the pan and seal on both sides. Lower the heat and cook for 3 minutes on each side.

For The Chickpea Purée

Heat the oil in a saucepan and sauté the garlic. Add the chickpeas and season with salt and cumin.

Spoon into a food processor, add the yoghurt and blend to a smooth purée. Pass through a fine sieve and keep warm.

For The Lamb Jus

Preheat the oven to 220°C (fan).

Place the lamb bones and trim into a roasting tray. Brown in the oven until crispy.

Remove the excess fat from the bones and place in a stockpot with the vegetables. Cover with cold water and cook for 3 hours. Strain and reduce to 200ml. Adjust the seasoning and finish with butter.

To Serve

Heat the beans in the butter, then add the diced feta. When warmed through, add the chickpeas and lovage.

Place the lamb belly onto warmed plates. Spoon the chickpea purée next to the lamb.

Arrange the bean and feta mix to the other side of the plate and finish with a drizzle of lamb jus. Garnish with radish.

Chef's Tip

The green beans and feta combination works really well as a lovely summer or vegetarian dish.

RASPBERRY, PEACH & ELDERFLOWER DOUGHNUTS

SERVES 8

🍷 *Coteaux du Layon St Lambert, Domaine Ogereau, Loire Valley, (France)*

Ingredients

Meringue

100g egg whites (about 3 egg whites)
100g caster sugar
100g icing sugar

Lemon Curd

500ml full-fat milk
250ml double cream
25ml lemon juice

Compressed Peaches

2 white peaches
100ml sweet white wine

Raspberry Gel

250g raspberry purée
75g caster sugar
25g agar agar
20ml lemon juice

Elderflower Doughnuts

125g ricotta
25g sugar
30ml elderflower cordial
1 lemon (zest of)
2 eggs
1 tsp baking powder
95g plain flour
caster sugar (to coat)
oil (to deep fry)

Raspberry Sorbet

150g sugar
150ml water
50ml lemon juice
500g raspberry purée

To Serve

1 punnet raspberries
2 peaches
elderflowers
2 tbsp freeze-dried raspberries

Method

For The Meringue (Prepare the day before)
Preheat the oven to 80°C (fan).
Whisk the ingredients together in a *bain-marie* for 5-7 minutes. Place into a freestanding mixer and whisk to stiff peaks. Spread onto baking paper on a tray and bake for 7 hours, or overnight until crisp. Break into shards.

For The Lemon Curd (Prepare the day before)
Pour the cream and milk into a pan and bring to 83°C on a low heat. Stir the lemon juice gently into the cream and bring up to 89°C.
Remove from the heat and allow to set for 15-20 minutes in the pan. Pass through a muslin cloth and keep in the fridge overnight until the texture becomes firm.

For The Compressed Peaches
Cut the peaches in half and remove the stones. Cut each half into 7 pieces. Place into a vac pack bag and add the wine. Vac pack the peach pieces and leave in the fridge for 2-3 hours.

> **Chef's Tip**
> If you can't compress the peaches, roast them with a dusting of icing sugar and olive oil to intensify the flavour.

To Make The Raspberry Gel
Bring the raspberry purée and sugar to the boil. Whisk in the agar agar and lemon juice and simmer for 2 minutes. Strain into a bowl, cling film the surface and cool in the fridge. Once set, blend to a smooth paste and store in a bottle.

To Make The Elderflower Doughnuts
Combine the ricotta, sugar, lemon zest and elderflower cordial. When smooth, beat in the eggs, one at a time. Fold in the flour and baking powder. Roll into mouth-sized balls.
Deep fry at 185°C for 2-3 minutes until golden. Drain on kitchen towel and place in a bowl. Add a dash of elderflower cordial, then roll in caster sugar until well coated.

For The Raspberry Sorbet
Bring the sugar, water and lemon juice to the boil, then stir in the raspberry purée. Chill over ice to 5°C. Churn in an ice cream machine until frozen.

To Serve
Place a few dots of raspberry gel on the plate. Coat half of the raspberries in the gel and arrange randomly, along with segments of fresh and compressed peach. Dot the lemon curd on the plate and stand the meringue shards in the droplets. Add a *quenelle* of sorbet and garnish with freeze-dried raspberries and elderflowers. Serve the doughnuts on the side.

208
THORESBY HALL HOTEL

Thoresby Hall Hotel & Spa, Near Ollerton, Nottingham, NG22 9WH

01623 821 000
www.warnerleisurehotels.co.uk/hotels/thoresby-hall-hotel

Thoresby Hall is a magnificent, plush and yet contemporary setting, serving the most amazing steaks, lobster and poultry with desserts to talk about until the cows come home!

Boasting a fabulous 2 AA Rosette, sumptuous afternoon teas and one of the UK's finest spas, Thoresby Hall has so much to offer.

The Blue Grill menu highlights its most popular starters - posh lobster fish finger or the sharing platter, a taster of their starters in miniature. Hand massaged Wagyu steaks from South Yorkshire are a feature of the menu, as are the lobster dishes or lemon sole and 'Fairground Attraction' dessert. A great value wine list complements the Grill menu.

Thoresby is a truly fabulous setting for a memorable evening; The Blue Grill was restored to replicate the grandeur of the original house. The walls are dressed with blue silk damask and the elegant 30 foot ceiling boasts views over the stunning grounds of the architectural delight that is Thoresby Hall.

Look out for a sumptuous riot of bays and balconies, gables and galleries.

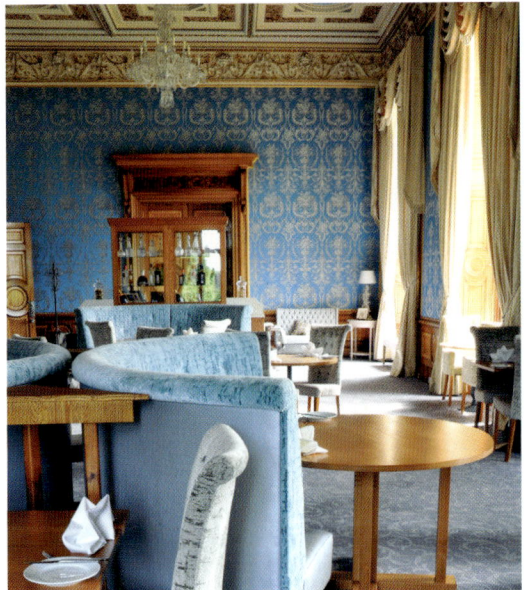

It is a sublime slice of Grade 1 listed revival exuberance, as good as you'll find in the whole of Britain let alone here at the edge of glorious and ancient Sherwood Forest.

Guests are assured of a warm welcome by the Thoresby team and general manager James Harding, and the very best of what The Blue Grill has to offer.

Award-winning executive chef Gary Griffiths proudly leads the team at The Blue Grill, serving some of the finest food the Midlands has to offer. He recommends you visit sometime very soon for the best steak around.

SMOKED DUCK BREAST, ROAST BEETROOT, BEETROOT JELLY

SERVES 4

🍷 *Rongopai Marlborough Sauvignon Blanc (New Zealand)*

Ingredients

Smoked Duck Breast

2 duck breasts
20g smoking chips
1g salt
1g pepper

Beetroot Jelly

200g beetroot (peeled, finely chopped)
½ litre water
50ml red wine vinegar
20g sugar
10g salt
2 leaves gelatine (softened)

Roast Beetroot

200g baby beetroot
5g thyme
5g garlic
salt (pinch of)

Red Wine Dressing (whisk ingredients together)

10ml olive oil
5ml Cabernet Sauvignon red wine vinegar
salt and pepper

Beetroot Purée

200g beetroot (peeled, finely chopped)
½ litre water
50ml red wine vinegar
20g sugar
10g salt

Croquettes

200g Ratte potatoes
40g smoked cheddar cheese
10g plain flour
2 eggs (beaten with 10ml milk)
30g fresh breadcrumbs

Garnish

baby shoots

Method

For The Smoked Duck Breast

Preheat the oven to 180ºC.

Place a large tray over a low heat with the smoking chips inside. Fit a steamer on top with the duck breasts in and cover with a lid. Smoke the breasts for 10 minutes. Once smoked, remove from the tray and season.

Render the duck breasts in a warm pan, skin-side down, until golden brown. Turn them over and repeat on the other side. Cook in the oven for 4 minutes.

> **Chef's Tip**
> Score the skin on the duck breast and seal in a warm pan to render down all of the fat.

For The Beetroot Jelly

Put the beetroot, water, vinegar, sugar and salt in a saucepan and bring to the boil. Once the beetroot is soft, remove from the heat and drain, catching the cooking liquor.

Place the beetroot into a blender, adding some of the liquid, and blend until smooth. Add the gelatine to the beetroot mix, pass through a sieve and set in a small tray. Cut into cubes.

For The Roast Beetroot

Preheat the oven to 160ºC.

Using some foil, make a bag and place the beetroot inside with the thyme, garlic and salt.

Roast the beetroot for 30 minutes until soft, then gently remove the skin. Portion and marinate in the red wine dressing.

For The Beetroot Purée

Bring all the ingredients to the boil in a saucepan, then simmer until soft. Remove from the heat and drain - catching the cooking liquor. Place the beetroot into a blender, adding some of the liquid and blend until smooth. Pass through a sieve and season.

For The Croquettes

Place the potatoes in cold water and cook with a pinch of salt until soft. Drain, then leave to steam to let the excess liquid out. Mash through a sieve and season. Add the grated cheese to the mash and shape into croquettes. *Pane,* then keep in the fridge. Deep fry at 180ºC until golden.

To Assemble The Dish

Place a swipe of beetroot purée onto a plate. Slice the duck breast and place on top. Dot cubes of jelly and roasted beetroot around the plate. Add the croquette and garnish with baby shoots. Place a cloche over the dish and fill with smoke using a smoke gun.

BEEF FILLET, TRIPLE COOKED CHIPS, MUSHROOM PUREE, BEARNAISE SAUCE

SERVES 4

Chateauneuf Du Pape Cuvee L'Hospice
Rhône Valley (France)

Ingredients

Beef

4 beef fillets
5ml olive oil
1g sea salt
1g pepper

Mushroom Purée

500g mushrooms
20g butter
10g thyme (chopped)
1 clove garlic (finely chopped)
20g shallots (diced)
30ml brandy
50ml double cream
10g Dijon mustard
10g tomato purée
10g salt
10g pepper

Triple Cooked Chips

500g potatoes
2g salt
2g pepper
oil (to deep fry)

Béarnaise Sauce

100g unsalted butter
25ml white wine vinegar
20g shallots (diced)
5 peppercorns
6g bay leaves
20g fresh tarragon
4 egg yolks
5ml lemon juice

Garnish

watercress
micro shoots

Method

For The Beef

Season the steak on all sides and coat in olive oil. Place onto a chargrill and seal all sides. Cook for 7 minutes, then rest.

For The Mushroom Purée

Sauté the mushrooms in butter with the thyme, garlic and shallots. Add the brandy and reduce until nearly evaporated. Stir in the cream, Dijon mustard and tomato purée and check the seasoning.
Cook the mixture down, then blend to a smooth purée.

For The Triple Cooked Chips

Cut the potatoes into chips and place in a bowl under running water for 5 minutes to wash the starch off.
Place the chips into cold tap water in a large saucepan.
Place the pan over a medium heat and simmer until the chips are almost falling apart, about 20-30 minutes, depending on the potato.
Carefully remove the cooked chips and place them on a cooling rack to dry out. Place in the freezer for at least 1 hour to remove more moisture.
Fry the chips in small batches until a light crust forms, about 5 minutes. Remove from the oil and drain on kitchen paper. Lay the potatoes on a cooling rack and place in the freezer for at least 1 hour. At this stage, if you don't want to cook and serve immediately, the chips can be kept frozen.
Heat the oil in the deep-fat fryer or deep pan to 180°C and fry the chips until golden, approximately 7 minutes. Drain and sprinkle with sea salt and pepper.

For The Béarnaise Sauce

Clarify the butter and leave to room temperature.
Reduce the vinegar with the shallots, peppercorns, tarragon trimmings and bay leaves.
Whisk the egg yolks over a *bain-marie* until starting to thicken, then add the strained vinegar and continue to whisk until thick and pale.
Add the *clarified butter* slowly whilst whisking to form a hollandaise. Add the chopped tarragon and a squeeze of lemon juice. Check the seasoning.

> **Chef's Tip**
> For the béarnaise sauce, infuse the tarragon stalks in the vinegar to add a depth of flavour.

To Serve

Serve as pictured.

CHOCOLATE PLANT POT MOUSSE, CHOCOLATE SOIL, MARSHMALLOWS

SERVES 4

Muscat De Beuume, Rhône Valley
(France)

Ingredients

Chocolate Plant Pot Mousse

50g sugar
200g dark chocolate
2 egg yolks
4 egg whites

Vanilla Ice Cream

400ml full-fat milk
1 fat vanilla pod (sliced lengthways, scraped)
4 egg yolks
75g caster sugar

Marshmallows (makes more than needed)

100ml water
500g sugar
10g glucose
7 leaves gelatine (softened)
4 egg whites
cornflour (to dust)

Chocolate Soil

100g sugar
10ml water
70g dark chocolate

To Serve

dark chocolate (melted)
edible flowers
8 raspberries (cut into quarters)

4 miniature plant pots

Method

For The Chocolate Plant Pot Mousse

Grind the sugar for 10 seconds, speed 10, in a Thermomix. Add the chocolate, then cream for 4 minutes, 50°C, speed 4. Add the yolks, 15 seconds, speed 4. Place the whisk and whisk for 3 minutes, speed 3.5. Fold the whites and chocolate together, pour the mousse into the plant pots, then set in the fridge for 2 hours.

Alternatively, use a normal mixer, melting the chocolate first and whisk the whites separately.

For The Vanilla Ice Cream

Place the vanilla pod and seeds in a pan with the milk. Bring the mixture almost to the boil, then remove from the heat.

Beat the egg yolks and caster sugar until light and fluffy. Fish the vanilla pod out and pour the milk through a sieve into the egg yolks and sugar, stirring until you get a thin custard. Pour into a clean saucepan and slowly bring the custard to the boil over a medium heat, stirring continuously with a wooden spoon. Remove from the heat when the mix coats the back of a spoon and leave to cool slightly. Churn in an ice cream machine until almost frozen.

For The Marshmallows

Boil the water, sugar and glucose to 125°C, then add the gelatine.

Whisk the egg whites to a soft peak. Combine all the ingredients together and set in a mould for at least 1 hour. Once set, remove, shape and dust in cornflour.

For The Chocolate Soil

Boil the water and sugar together to 130°C. Place the chocolate into a mixer and pour the sugar in slowly until it forms 'soil'.

To Serve

Swipe the plates with a little melted, dark chocolate. Roll a ball of ice cream in some soil and plate along with the chocolate pot. Garnish with the soil, marshmallow, raspberries and edible flowers.

> **Chef's Tip**
> Take the chocolate plant pots out a couple of hours before serving so they are at room temperature when eating.

CALLING ALL CHEFS! ISN'T IT ABOUT TIME YOU FEATURED IN ONE OF OUR BOOKS?

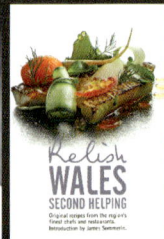

Relish Publications is an independent publishing house based in north east England. The business was founded on an award-winning series of restaurant guides and recipe books featuring each region across England, Scotland and Wales. Relish has now worked with over 1,500 leading chefs and restaurants, building a portfolio of beautifully illustrated guides which are stocked nationally in Waterstones, Harvey Nichols, in each featured restaurant, in leading independent stores and online globally.

Relish has a small, friendly professional team, with experience in publishing, print management, editing, proofing, photography, design and artwork, sales distribution and marketing.

Relish Publications ensure a personal approach to every single customer, working exceptionally hard to develop a great product which reflects each chef's talent and passion.

Duncan and Teresa Peters established the company in 2009, with a vision of building a niche publishing house for food lovers. The success of Relish is now reflected in the fact that they have an ongoing programme of regional books, with many regions now having a Second and Third Helping (edition) of the leading restaurant guide and dozens of independent commissions from internationally celebrated chefs including Jean Christophe Novelli.

To find out how your chef or restaurant can be featured or discuss your publishing requirements simply log on to our publishing website www.relish-publishing.co.uk or call our head office on 01670 571 635 and speak to one of our team.

219
HINTS & TIPS...

HOW TO MAKE ICE CREAM WITHOUT A MACHINE

Although relatively inexpensive these days, not everyone has access to an ice cream machine. That's no reason not to follow some of these delicious recipes found in the Relish Midlands book. Although more time consuming than a machine, excellent results can be obtained by following this simple method.

Follow the recipe right up until it tells you to churn in the machine, including any chilling time in the fridge.

Take your mixture from the fridge and stir with a rubber spatula. Transfer it to a suitable plastic container with a lid. There should be at least 2cm space at the top to allow the mixture to expand when freezing. Cover and place in the freezer for two hours.

Remove from the freezer and beat with a hand mixer, still in the container, to break up the ice crystals that are beginning to form. Cover and return to the freezer for a further 2 hours. (If you don't have a hand mixer then you may use a fork and some 'elbow grease' to break up the crystals).

Remove from the freezer and beat again with the hand mixer. The ice cream should be thickening up nicely at this point but too soft to scoop. Return it to the freezer for an additional hour. Beat again. If your ice cream is still not thickened sufficiently, repeat this process again after another hour. When the ice cream has thickened properly, stir in any add-ins at this point (honeycomb, nuts...). Do not beat with the hand mixer after the add-ins have been mixed in.

Place the tightly sealed container in the freezer and allow the ice cream to freeze until firm. The ice cream should be removed from the freezer 15-20 minutes before you wish to eat it. This will make scooping easier.

This method will also work for sorbets. Sometimes sorbets may go a bit 'icy' or 'crumbly' if left for too long in the freezer. This can be rectified by blitzing in a food processor just before serving.

Mr Gibbons' Sticky Toffee Pudding, Butterscotch Sauce, Vanilla Ice Cream - **Page 076**

HOW TO MAKE A SUGAR STOCK SYRUP

This makes about 750ml sugar stock. It can be stored in a sterilised jar in the fridge for a couple of months.

500g white sugar
500ml water

Place the sugar and water in a pan. Dissolve slowly over a very low heat. You must not allow the syrup to boil until all the sugar has dissolved, about 5 minutes. Once completely dissolved, bring to the boil, then simmer for 5 minutes.

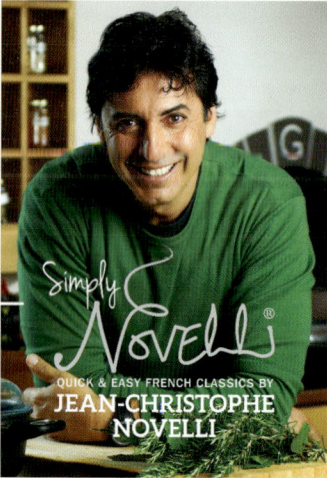

Simply
Novelli®
QUICK & EASY FRENCH CLASSICS BY
JEAN-CHRISTOPHE
NOVELLI

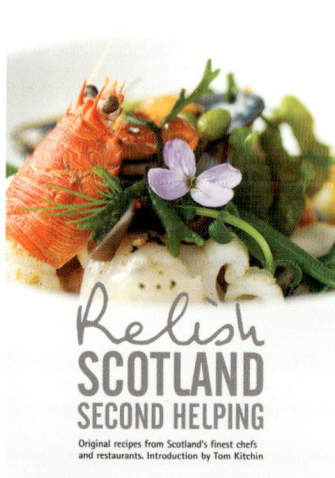

Relish
SCOTLAND
SECOND HELPING

Original recipes from Scotland's finest chefs
and restaurants. Introduction by Tom Kitchin

Relish
COTSWOLDS &
OXFORDSHIRE

Original recipes from the Cotswolds and
Oxfordshire's finest chefs and restaurants

Relish
**NORTH EAST
& YORKSHIRE**

Original recipes from the North East
and Yorkshire's finest chefs and
restaurants. Introduction by celebrity chefs
James Martin and Hairy Biker, Si King.

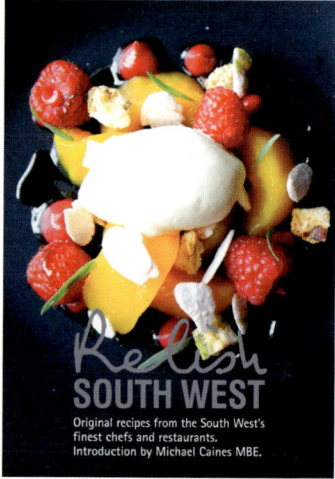

Relish
SOUTH WEST

Original recipes from the South West's
finest chefs and restaurants.
Introduction by Michael Caines MBE.

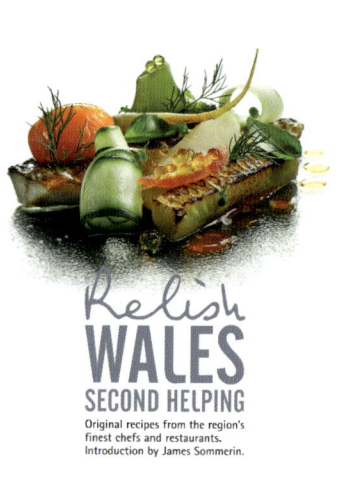

Relish
WALES
SECOND HELPING

Original recipes from the region's
finest chefs and restaurants.
Introduction by James Sommerin.

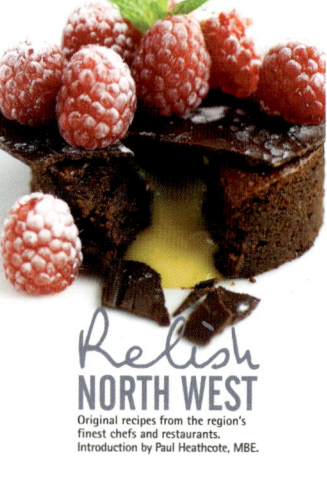

Relish
NORTH WEST

Original recipes from the region's
finest chefs and restaurants.
Introduction by Paul Heathcote, MBE.

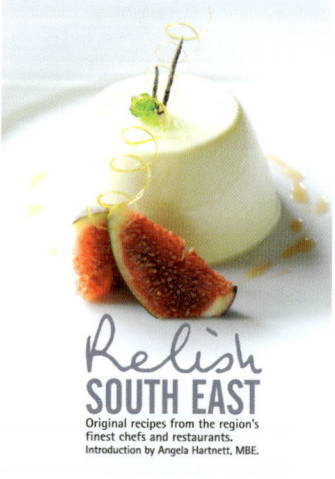

Relish
SOUTH EAST

Original recipes from the region's
finest chefs and restaurants.
Introduction by Angela Hartnett, MBE.

Relish
SCOTLAND
THIRD HELPING

Original recipes from the region's finest chefs
and restaurants. Featuring the Michelin starred
chefs of Scotland.

HERE'S WHAT SOME OF BRITAIN'S BEST CHEFS HAVE SAID ABOUT WORKING WITH RELISH

"Relish books are full of enjoyable recipes and ideas for making the most edible treasures we have on our doorstep; both places to eat them and new, exciting ways to cook them."
Angela Hartnett, MBE

"The Relish cookbook offers the home cook some great inspiration to make the most of these wonderful ingredients in season." *Tom Kitchin, The Kitchin, Edinburgh*

"With mouth-watering, easy to follow recipes and beautiful photography, this book is a must have for any foodie, from professional chef to the inspired home cook."
Michael Caines MBE

"Relish brings together some of the most talented chefs from the regions. It shines the spotlight on the exceptional ways in which fresh, seasonal, local ingredients are put to good use." *Gary Jones, Executive Head Chef, Le Manoir aux Quat'Saisons*

"I'm immensely proud to be writing the foreword to a book that celebrates the best of Midland's food."
Andreas Antona, Simpsons Restaurant, Birmingham

"The Relish team has truly been amazing to work with. To have produced my book within two months from start to finish, only shows how professional a team of people can be."
Jean-Christophe Novelli

222
LARDER

MEAT & POULTRY

19 GALES FARM
Bentley, Atherstone, Warwickshire, CV9 2JR.
T: 01827 716 551 or 716 758 www.19gales.co.uk

AUBREY ALLEN
Unit 1, 3040 Siskin Parkway East, Coventry, CV3 4PE.
T: 02476 422 222 www.aubreyallenwholesale.co.uk

D W WALL & SON
Corvedale Road, Craven Arms, Shropshire, SY7 9NL.
T: 01588 672 308 www.wallsbutchers.co.uk

FOREST PIG CHARCUTERIE
Bell Farm, Far Forest, Worcestershire, DY14 9DX.
T: 01299 266 771 www.forestpig.com

HOUGH & SONS
16 Beaumont Road, Church Stretton, SY6 6BN.
T: 01694 722 386

OWEN TAYLOR & SON
27 Main Road, Leabrooks, Derbyshire, DE55 1LA.
T: 01773 603 351 www.owentaylor.co.uk

SWAINSON HOUSE FARM
Goosnargh Lane, Goosnargh, Preston PR3 2JU.
T: 01772 865 251 www.jandsgoosnargh.co.uk

FISH

FLYING FISH SEAFOOD
Unit 9 & 10, Indian Queens Workshops, Cornwall, TR9 6JP.
T: 01726 862 876 www.flyingfishseafoods.co.uk

KELYNACK CORNISH FISH
2C Willis Vean Industrial Estate, Mullion, Helston,
Cornwall, TR12 7DF.
T: 01326 241 373 www.kelynackcornishfish.com

M & J SEAFOOD
Potterton Way, Smethwick, West Midlands, B66 1AU.
T: 0844 800 4545 www.mjseafood.com

FRUIT & VEG

HAMPTON FARM SHOP
Pershore Road, Evesham, Worcestershire, WR11 2NB.
T: 01386 41540

WORCESTER PRODUCE
Ascot Rd, Pershore, Worcestershire, WR10 2JJ.
T: 01386 562 402 www.worcesterproduce.co.uk

ROWLANDS & CO
Shrewsbury, Knights Way, Battlefield Enterprise Park,
Shrewsbury, SY1 3AB.
T: 01743 462 244 www.rowlandsltd.co.uk

SPECIALITY & FINE FOODS

HARVEY & BROCKLESS, THE FINE FOOD COMPANY
Broomhall Farm, Broomhall, Worcester, WR5 2NT
www.harveyandbrockless.co.uk

TURNERS FINE FOODS
Unit 7, Spelmonden Farm, Goudhurst, Kent, TN17 1HE.
T: 01580 212 818 www.turnersfinefoods.com

WELLOCKS
4 Pendleside, Lomeshaye Business Village, Lancashire,
BB9 6SH. T: 08444 993 444 www.wellocks.co.uk

DRY & FROZEN GOODS

BIKOLD FOODSERVICE
Lingen Road, Ludlow Business Park, Ludlow, Shropshire,
SY8, 1XD. T: 01584 877 866 www.bikold.co.uk

WINES

PAUL ROBERTS WINES
Lawden Road, Bordesley, Birmingham, B10 0AD.
T: 0121 773 8249 www.paulrobertswines.co.uk

FARM SHOP

BEWDLEY FARM SHOP
Dog Lane, Bewdley, Worcestershire, DY12 2EF.
T: 01299 400 346 www.bewdleyfarmshop.co.uk

DAIRY

MAWLEY TOWN FARM DAIRIES
Cleobury Mortimer, Kidderminster, DY14 8PJ.
T: 01299 270 359 www.mawleytownfarm.co.uk

223
GLOSSARY

BAIN-MARIE
A pan or other container of hot water with a bowl placed on top of it. This allows the steam from the water to heat the bowl so ingredients can be gently heated or melted.

BALLOTINE
A deboned leg of a chicken, duck or other poultry stuffed with ground meat and other ingredients, tied and cooked.

BEURRE NOISETTE
Unsalted butter is melted over a low heat until it begins to caramelise and brown. When it turns a nutty colour, it should be removed from the heat to stop it burning. Can be used as a base for butter sauces or added to cakes and batters.

BLANCH
Boiling an ingredient before removing it and plunging it in ice cold water in order to stop the cooking process.

BRUNOISE
A type of culinary cut in which food is diced into 3.175mm cubes. The formal-looking little squares add colour and elegance to dishes.

CHIFFONADE
A chopping technique in which herbs or leafy green vegetables (such as spinach and basil) are cut into long, thin strips.

CHINOIS
A conical sieve with an extremely fine mesh. It is used to strain custards, purées, soups and sauces, producing a very smooth texture.

CLARIFIED BUTTER/CLARIFYING
Milk fat rendered from butter to separate the milk solids and water from the butter fat.

CONCASSE
To roughly chop any ingredient, usually vegetables, most specifically applied to tomatoes, with tomato concasse being a tomato that has been peeled and seeded (seeds and skins removed).

CONFIT
A method of cooking where the meat is cooked and submerged in a liquid to add flavour. Often this liquid is rendered fat. Confit can also apply to fruits - fruit confits are cooked and preserved in sugar, the result is like candied fruits.

EMULSION/EMULSIFY
In the culinary arts, an emulsion is a mixture of two liquids that would ordinarily not mix together, like oil and vinegar.

FRENCH TRIMMED
To French trim, fat, meat or skin is cut away to expose a piece of bone, so that it sticks out.
It also means that any excess fat is cut off. French Trimming can be done to lamb chops and bigger cuts; it can even can be done to chicken legs or breasts.

ITALIAN MERINGUE
Made by beating egg whites until they reach soft, fluffy peaks, then slowly streaming in boiling sugar and beating the mixture until it is thick and glossy.

JULIENNE
A culinary knife cut in which the vegetable is sliced into long thin strips, similar to matchsticks.

MACERATE
Raw, dried, or preserved fruit and vegetables soaked in a liquid to soften the food or to absorb the flavour.

PANE
To coat with flour, beaten egg and breadcrumbs for deep frying.

QUENELLE
A neat, three-sided oval (resembling a mini rugby ball) that is formed by gently smoothing the mixture between two dessert spoons.

SOUS VIDE
French for 'under vacuum.' A method of cooking food sealed in airtight plastic bags in a water bath or in a temperature-controlled steam environment for longer than normal cooking times. The intention is to cook the item evenly, ensuring that the inside is properly cooked without overcooking the outside, and to retain moisture.

CONVERSION CHART

COOKING TEMPERATURES

Degrees Celsius	Fahrenheit	Gas Mark
140	275	1
150	300	2
160-170	325	3
180	350	4
190	375	5
200-210	400	6
220	425	7
230	450	8
240	475	9

*Temperatures for fan-assisted ovens are, as a general rule, normally about 20°C lower than regular oven temperature.

WEIGHT MEASUREMENT CONVERSIONS

1 teaspoon (5ml/5g)	$1/4$ oz
1 tablespoon (15ml/15g)	$3/4$ oz
10g	$1/2$ oz
25g	1oz
50g	2oz
75g	3oz
150g	5oz
200g	7oz
250g	9oz
350g	12oz
450g	1lb
1kg	2.2lb

VOLUME MEASUREMENT CONVERSIONS

55ml	2 fl oz
150ml	$1/4$ pt
275ml	$1/2$ pint
570ml	1 pt
1 litre	$1 3/4$ pt

Relish
MIDLANDS
SECOND HELPING

Original recipes from the region's finest chefs
and restaurants. Introduction by Adam Stokes.

First Published 2015
By Relish Publications
Shield Green Farm, Tritlington,
Northumberland, NE61 3DX.

Twitter: @Relish_Cookbook
Facebook: RelishRestaurantGuide
For cookbooks and recipes visit:
www.relishpublications.co.uk
For publishing enquiries visit:
www.relish-publishing.co.uk

ISBN: 978-0-9575370-9-5

Publisher: Duncan L Peters
General Manager: Teresa Peters
Design: Vicki Brown
Relish Photography: Andy Richardson
www.awaywithmedia.com Twitter: @andyrichardson1
Editorial Consultant: Paul Robertson
Proofing Coordinator: Valerie McLeod
Sales: Wendy Rutterford
Coordinator: Rebecca Laycock

Front cover photograph by: Andy Richardson

Printed in Poland on behalf of Latitude Press

Relish
PUBLICATIONS